JUNG

AND

HESSE

A Record of
Two
Friendships

Miguel Serrano

SCHOCKEN BOOKS
NEW YORK

JUNG
AND
HESSE

One of Hesse's illustrations for *Piktor's Metamorphosis*.

Contents

HERMANN HESSE

C. G. JUNG

v

Contents

Illustrations

Acknowledgements

The letters, drawings and poems of Hermann Hesse are published by permission of Mrs. Ninon Hesse.

The letters of C. G. Jung are published by permission of his family and will also be published in the *Collected Letters of Jung* edited by Gerhard Adler. They were written in English and are reproduced here as in the original except for minor corrections of punctuation and idiom.

Hermann Hesse

_____

On January 22, 1961, I had lunch with Hermann Hesse at his house in Montagnola, in the Italian section of Switzerland. Snowflakes were fluttering by the window, but in the distance, the sky was bright and clear. As I turned away from the view, I caught the clear blue eyes of Hesse sitting at the far end of the table.

'What luck,' I said, 'to find myself lunching with you today.'

'Nothing ever happens by chance,' he answered. 'Here only the right guests meet. This is the Hermetic Circle. . . .'

Demian

I FIRST DISCOVERED the works of Hermann Hesse in about 1945. At that time, he was almost unknown in Chile, appreciated only in the coteries and discussed almost furtively. Indeed, before 1946, Hesse had hardly any reputation at all outside of Germany. In that year, however, he was given the Nobel Prize for literature, and subsequently his works have been translated into many languages. Even so, his books are received enthusiastically in only a few countries. The Anglo-Saxon world, for example, considers him to be heavy and dull, and for this reason, his complete works have never been published in English. Once when I was in London, I had to look for days to find some of his best-known works in order to give them to a friend of mine who was literate but who had never heard of Hesse. In the Spanish-speaking world, the situation is quite different, however, and Hesse has been so widely and repeatedly read that the young people of Spain and South America virtually consider him as a prophet.

Once, a Mexican painter gave me a colour slide of a painting of his depicting the Magister Musicae and Josef Knecht in Hesse's *Magister Ludi*. The old teacher is shown at the piano, and young Knecht accompanies him on the violin in the first sonata they played together. The Mexican had been so excited by the book that he had not only made the painting, but had sent it to Hesse as a gift.

This enthusiasm of the Mexican painter is quite easy for me to understand. Even today, I would go half-way round the world to find a book if I thought it essential to my needs, and I have a feeling of absolute veneration for those few authors who have given me something special. For this reason I can never understand the tepid youth of today who wait for books to be given to them and who neither search nor admire. I would go without eating in order to get a book, and I have never liked borrowing books, because I have always wanted them to be absolutely mine so that I could live with them for hours on end.

As with men, it has always seemed to me that books have their own peculiar destinies. They go towards the people who are waiting for them and reach them at the right moment. They are made of living material and continue to cast light through the darkness long after the death of their authors.

The first of Hesse's books which I read was *Demian*. It made an extraordinary impression on me and gave me a strength which I had never found before. The edition I read was a Spanish translation, and it probably contained many errors; nevertheless the magic and the energy remained. While still young, and living in the Pension Verenahof in Baden, Hesse had concentrated such force into it that it was still alive and vital many years later.

The hero Demian was destined to influence many lives, and undoubtedly hundreds have tried to emulate his strength and serenity. After reading it, I myself used to wander through the streets of my city feeling myself a new man, the bearer of a message and a sign. Thus Hesse has always been more than a literary man or a poet, not only for me but for whole generations of men. His magical books delve into regions that are usually reserved for religion, and these are the ones that are important for me—*Demian*, *The Journey to the East*, the fantastic *Autobiography*, *Siddhartha*, *Magister Ludi*, *Steppenwolf* and *Death and the Lover*.

Demian is not actually a physical being, since he is never separated from Sinclair, the character who narrates the book. In fact, Demian is Sinclair himself, his deepest self, a kind of archetypal hero who exists in the depths of all of us. In a word, Demian is the essential Self which remains unchanging and untouched, and through him the book attempts to give instruction concerning the magical essence of existence. Demian provides the young boy Sinclair with a redeeming awareness of the millennial being which exists within him so that he can overcome chaos and danger, especially during the years of adolescence. In our own lives, many of us have encountered people like Demian, those young men who are sure of themselves and who consequently earn our respect and admiration. But in fact Demian resides within all of us. At the end of the book, Demian approaches Sinclair, who is lying on a bed at a field hospital, and as he kisses him, he says, 'Listen, little one, if you ever need me again, do not expect me to come back so openly on a horse or in a train. Look for me within yourself.' Hesse wrote this at a time of great personal anguish, when he was about to abandon his country because of the war that had enveloped all of Europe. He had been forced to find Demian within himself.

This message is not literally specified within the book; rather it is hinted at magically. Moreover, this symbolic truth can only be understood intuitively, but when it appears, it enlightens the whole being, and that is why many years ago I was able to walk through the streets of my city, feeling that something new had come into my life.

Abraxas

ALTHOUGH LIFE IS AN AFFAIR of light and shadows, we never accept it as such. We are always reaching towards the light and the high peaks. From childhood, through early religious and academic training, we are given values which correspond only to an ideal world. The shadowy side of real life is ignored, and Western Christianity provides us with nothing which can be used to interpret it. Thus the young men of the West are unable to deal with the mixture of light and shadow of which life really consists; they have no way of linking the facts of existence to their preconceived notions of absolutes. The links connecting life with universal symbols are therefore broken, and disintegration sets in.

In the Orient, and especially in India, the situation is very different. There, an ancient civilization based on nature accepts a cosmos of multi-faceted gods; and thus the Easterner can realize the simultaneous existence of light and shadow and of good and evil. Absolutes do not exist, and if God is thus disarmed, so is the devil. But the price of such an understanding is a direct tribute to nature itself. Consequently, the Hindu finds himself less individualized than the Westerner; he is little more than a part of nature, one element in the collective soul.

The question which the Western Christian now has to face is whether, without losing his individuality, he can accept the coexistence of light and shadow and of God and the devil. To do so, he will have to discover the God who was Christian before the personalized Christ and who can continue in a viable form after him. Such a deity would be the Christ of Atlantis, who once existed publicly, and who still continues to exist—even though submerged under the deep waters of our present civilization. Such a god would also be Abraxas, who is God and the devil at the same time.

The first time I heard of Abraxas by name was in *Demian*, but I had really known about him from my childhood days. I had sensed his existence in the heart of the Cordillera of the Andes and in the unfathomable depths of the Pacific Ocean which beats against our coasts. This *ignis fatuus*, the flames of heaven and hell which exist in him, flickered even in the foam of these waves.

Abraxas is a Gnostic god who existed long before Christ. He may be equated too with the Christ of Atlantis, and is known by other names by the aborigines of the Americas, amongst them the Indians who inhabited my country.

Hermann Hesse speaks of him in this way:

> Contemplate the fire, contemplate the clouds, and when omens appear and voices begin to sound in your soul, abandon yourself to them without wondering beforehand whether it seems convenient or good to do so. If you hesitate, you will spoil your own being, you will become little more than the bourgeois façade which encloses you, and you will become a fossil. Our god is named Abraxas, and he is both god and the devil at the same time. You will find in him both the world of light and of shadows. Abraxas is not opposed to any of your thoughts or to any of your dreams, but he will abandon you if you become normal and unapproachable. He will abandon you and look for another pot in which to cook his thoughts.

The modern Christian and the Western world as a whole has now reached a point of crisis, and the choices open seem less than attractive. We neither want one of those apocolyptic catastrophes which have so disfigured our past history, nor do we want the de-humanizing path of the Orient which would result in an irremediable lowering of our standards. Perhaps then the only possibility that remains is Abraxas, that is to say, a projection of our souls both outwards and inwards, both to

1. The author with Hermann Hesse in Montagnola.

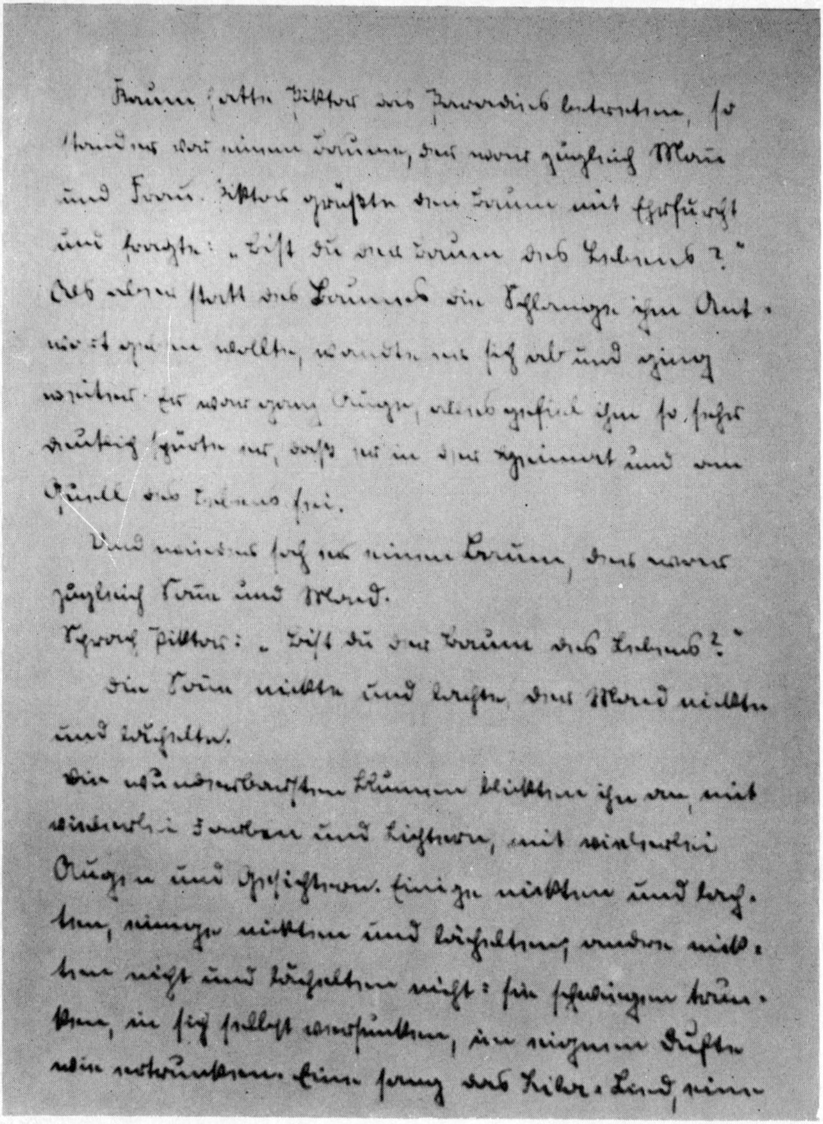

2. Example of Hermann Hesse's handwriting.

the light and to the deep shadows of our biographical roots, in hopes of finding in the combination of the two the pure archetype. This pure archetype would be the authentic image of the god which is within ourselves and which has been sunk for so long, like Atlantis, under the waters of our consciousness. Thus Abraxas would also come to mean Total Man.

Narcissus, Goldmund and Siddhartha

FOR THOSE FAMILIAR with Hesse's works, the names of Narcissus, Goldmund and Siddhartha are well known. They are also figures who have much in common, since Hesse's books contain a leitmotiv which is always the same. Thus, as Sinclair and Demian are the same person, so Narcissus and Goldmund represent two essential tendencies in man—contemplation and action. Similarly, Siddhartha and Govinda represent the opposed characteristics of devotion and rebellion. These are qualities contained in all of us individually; we love ourselves but we are also charitable towards others; we are torn between introspection and extroversion. *Magister Ludi* contains the themes of love, pity and understanding, and develops them into the fugues and arabesques which are so dear to the musical soul of the Germans. The concepts with which Hesse deals are influenced by Hinduism, Chinese Taoism, Zen Buddhism, and even mathematics, but they are worked together into a form as pure as a Bach fugue or a painting by Leonardo.

When I first met Hermann Hesse, I found him more like Narcissus than Goldmund. He had stopped wandering and was living a life of introspection in his isolated retreat at Montagnola. Nevertheless, both Narcissus and Goldmund continued to exist within him together until the end of his life. For myself, at that time I was more like Goldmund than Narcissus, although I too was torn between those two ways of being. And like Siddhartha, I was to meet this wise being many times, visiting him in various guises. For that first interview I was carrying an alpine knapsack and had a book under my arm. I was young, and it was the first time that I had ever left my own country.

When I first arrived in Switzerland, in June of 1951, I found that very few people knew where Hesse was staying, and it was only in Berne, after many inquiries, that I discovered his general whereabouts. I took the train to Lugano, where I made further inquiries, and was told that Hesse was living in Castagnola. I took a bus there only to find that Hesse's home was really in Montagnola. Another bus took me to that mountain town with its view of the snow-covered Alps and Lake Lugano. The bus climbed up through the narrow streets until at last it reached its destination. A young woman got off the bus with me, and I asked her if she knew where Hesse lived. She told me that she was his servant and asked me to follow her.

It was dusk by the time we reached the entrance to the garden. Over the gate there was a sign which read in German 'Bitte Keine Besuche'—No Visitors Permitted. I passed through after the servant girl and walked along a path bordered by tall trees. At the front door, there was yet another inscription in German which I later learned was a translation from old Chinese:

WORDS OF MENG-TSE

When a man has reached old age
And has fulfilled his mission,
He has a right to confront
The idea of death in peace.
He has no need of other men;
He knows them and knows enough about them.
What he needs is *peace*.
It isn't good to visit this man or to talk to him,
To make him suffer banalities.
One must give a wide berth
To the door of his house,
As if no one lived there.

At the time, it was too dark to read this inscription and so, when the girl opened the door and asked me to enter, I did so. She offered me a chair beside a small table in the dark passageway and asked me for my visiting card. I didn't have one, so I gave her my book, *Neither by Sea nor Land*. I had brought it specially for Hesse and had inscribed it for him in Spanish.

The girl went off down the passageway, and as I waited in that cloistered atmosphere, I had the feeling that I was enveloped in an aura of sandalwood. Then a side door opened and a slim figure dressed in white came out into the shadows. It was Hesse. I stood up, but I was unable to see him clearly until after we had left the passageway and entered a room with large windows. His eyes were very bright, and although his face was thin, he smiled openly. Dressed all in white, he looked like an ascetic or a penitent. I then realized that he was the source of the sandalwood perfume.

'I am sorry, but you have arrived at an awkward moment,' he said. 'We were supposed to have gone on vacation yesterday, but my wife was stung by a bee, and we have had to postpone our trip. Everything is topsy-turvy here, but let's go into my study.'

We crossed the living-room which had bookshelves reaching to the ceiling and entered another smaller room. In the centre was a desk, and here too the walls were lined with bookshelves and paintings. Hesse sat down with his back to the window, and I could see the sun setting over the mountains and lake in the distance. The desk had been cleared of papers, and I sat down next to it facing him. Hesse continued to smile but did not say a word. He seemed to be waiting for an atmosphere of peace to take possession of the room.

I felt the importance of the moment, and now, as I recount it, I realize that those were intense years in my life and that my whole being was then capable of trembling at a meeting; it was a time, indeed, when meetings still existed. There I was before the object of my veneration. I had crossed the seas to meet him, and the welcome that he gave me was in complete accord with the feelings with which I had begun my pilgrimage. It seemed to me that Hermann Hesse had no particular age. At that time, he had just turned seventy-three; but his smile was the smile of a young man, and his body seemed so spiritually disciplined that it was like a blade of fine steel sheathed in white linen.

'I have come a long way,' I began, 'but of course you are very well known in my country. . . .'

'It is strange that my books are read so much in the Spanish-speaking countries,' he answered. 'I often receive letters from Latin America. I wish you would tell me what you think of the new translations, especially the one of *Magister Ludi*.'

I told him what I thought and said that the translation of *Death and the Lover* preserved both the spirit and the sense of the original. We then began to speak of more general matters.

'Narcissus and Goldmund represent two contrary tendencies of the soul.' he said. 'These are contemplation and action. One day, however, they must begin to fuse. . . .'

'I know what you mean,' I broke in, 'because I too live within that tension and am caught between the two extremes. I dream of the peace of contemplation, but the necessity of living always pushes me into action. . . .'

'You should let yourself be carried away, like the clouds in the sky. You shouldn't resist. God exists in your destiny just as much as he does in these mountains and in that lake. It is very difficult to understand this, because man is moving further and further away from nature, and also from himself. . . .'

'Do you think the wisdom of Asia can be helpful?' I asked.

'I have been more inspired by the wisdom of China than by the Upanishads or the Vedanta,' he answered. 'The *I Ching* can transform a life. . . .'

Outside the late afternoon sky began to pale, and a tenuous blue light tinted the windows and played over Hesse's slight form.

'Tell me,' I asked, 'have you been able to find peace here in the mountains?'

Hesse remained silent for a time, although his soft smile never disappeared. We seemed to hear the gentle murmur of the afternoon light and the silence of things until at length he spoke:

'When you are close to nature you can listen to the voice of God.'

We remained seated there until at length I realized that it was time to leave. Hesse gave me a small watercolour which he had painted himself, and he wrote on the back, 'Ricordo di Montagnola'. He loved painting and was a good watercolourist. He accompanied me to the door and shook my hand like an old friend saying, 'If you come back another time, you may no longer find me here.'

That was how my first interview went. Those who are still young enough to ask questions like those I asked Hesse that afternoon, or like those that Siddhartha asked Buddha, will understand my impression.

On my return through the narrow streets of Montagnola I could not find a bus, but a young man took me to Lugano on his motor-cycle. That same night I found myself in Florence, that city so imbued with Renaissance magic. But those were the post-war years, and impoverished Italy was still seeking refuge in the dollar and in the alcohol of the occupation troops.

Cities and Years

MANY YEARS were to pass before I next met Hermann Hesse; nevertheless, in all that time we did not stop corresponding. For the most part, his messages were allusive and subtle. I can only marvel at the strangeness of our relationship. Although we were separated by years, continents, and cultural backgrounds, we were slowly to form such a true friendship that it seemed a thing of destiny. The world-famous writer, the Teacher and Magician, had stretched out his hand to a young and unknown writer who had come from a small country almost lost in the farthest corner of the world; and he made him his friend, even to the point of saying to him at the end of his days, 'I have no more friends of my own age left; I have only friends who are younger than myself.'

After I left for India in 1953, I began to receive more frequent communications from Hesse because, even though he was saturated with ancient Hindu widsom, he was still fascinated by the subject. I had not told him that I was going to India as a diplomat since I wanted to remain in his eyes as a pilgrim, the way I had first appeared to him with my staff and knapsack in Switzerland.

My life and experiences in India are recounted in my book, *The Serpent of Paradise*. I will only add here that not a year passed without my sending him something, or receiving something from that hermit who had said that he did not like to extend himself. Sometimes there were photographs, at other times paintings, poems or books. Once, on a newspaper clipping of an article of his about Tibet he wrote the Spanish words 'Saludos' next to his printed name. Ours certainly was not a literary friendship; rather it was a magical meeting across the barriers of time and space.

Montagnola is a small town high up over Lake Lugano and is made up of clean, narrow streets lined by well-cared-for houses, some of whose older houses have been reproduced by Hesse in his Ticino watercolours. For many years he had an apartment in an old house whose windows looked out over a wooded garden and rolling hills. On the balcony of that house he wrote *Klingsor's Last Summer*, a story which burns with the summer heat of that place.

I have often gone to sit on the stone steps in that garden and to look at the balcony and the curious parapets of the house. It had been built by one of the Swiss architects who had been mercenaries in the army with which Napoleon invaded Russia. After the long retreat, the mercenaries stayed behind to rebuild Moscow. Afterwards they returned to Switzerland as rich men and became moneyed proprietors. I have seen this beautiful house during the hot, dry summer days, and have also seen it covered with snow. I have watched the dry autumnal leaves fall from the plane trees that guard the front of the house, and I have also seen spring flowers sprouting in the garden.

In his latter years, Hesse lived in another house set by itself on a hill with a great orchard full of fruit and shade trees. It had been especially built for him by a friend who gave it to him until his death. It was in that house that our first interview had taken place, and it was there that I was to go again after so many years.

This time on the way to Montagnola, I passed through the beautiful Italian-Swiss cities of Locarno and Ascona. It was March 1, 1959, and nearly eight years had passed. I was now representing my country as Ambassador to India. This was a new incarnation, and Siddhartha was returning to meet his friend wearing different clothes.

The car climbed slowly up through the narrow streets of the town and finally stopped at the door of an inn. There I chatted with the owner, Mr. Ceccarelli, while his wife rang up Hesse's house to make an appointment for me. Hesse agreed to see me that same afternoon.

I walked up to the house and passed through the familiar gates and was soon seated in the large-windowed room. Once again I was with Hesse. He was now eighty years old, but his face was unchanged—although I imagined I saw traces of sadness in his smile.

For myself, I felt I was no longer the pilgrim I had been on the former visit. The hard climate of Asia and the busy years that had passed had left their mark on me. Nevertheless, I was deeply moved by this new encounter.

Mrs. Hesse came into the room, and I noticed that she was considerably younger than her husband. She was reserved, and her smile was somewhat withdrawn. Hesse began the conversation by asking me about current affairs in India. He then recalled his own visit to that country.

'The Indians are a great people; they seem to be made for suffering.' he said. 'I was in India years ago—my trip was an act of homage to my father and grandfather. My grandfather knew India well, and he brought back with him a little statue of Krishna which I have always loved. I also have a good friend in India, Professor Kalidasa Nath, who lived in Calcutta. I wonder if he is still alive. Perhaps you could find out for me when you go back, and if he is still living, give him my regards. He once visited me with Romain Rolland.'

I told him I would do so, and then said that I had brought a few things for him. I handed him a few sticks of sandalwood to burn and an old miniature from the Kangra Valley which showed two women walking along a dark path under the monsoon rains. One of the women was gently resting her hand on the shoulder of the other.

'Perhaps that is the princess Fatima,' I said, 'whom you were looking for in your book *The Journey to the East.*'

Hesse smiled and looked at the painting. He showed the miniature to his wife and pointed out the hand of the young girl resting on her friend's shoulder. 'That is a very sweet hand,' he murmured.

On the back of the painting, I had written: 'For Hermann Hesse, from the world of symbols.' I pointed this out to Hesse, and said, 'I wrote that because you have lived your own symbols and fable, and have developed and enlarged them in your writing.'

Mrs. Hesse went out of the room and then came back with a bottle of wine, which she placed on the table. Hesse rested the miniature against it and continued to look at it.

'I've just come from Locarno,' I said, 'where I saw Professor Jung. He too is fascinated by symbols, interpreting and analyzing them. I've always thought it strange that the Indians gavė so little importance to his work.'

'The reason for that,' answered Hesse, 'is that India doesn't interpret symbols; it lives them. Thus it has taken twenty years to have my own book, *Siddhartha*, published in India. It has only just been translated into Hindi, Bengali and several other Indian languages. And my book doesn't even interpret symbols. I have often thought of this Indian aloofness as a kind of "mental egotism"; nevertheless, there is a certain strength in it. Especially in contrast with Japan, where everything strange and foreign is immediately assimilated. This "mental egotism" is probably a necessary defence mechanism.'

'Yes,' I answered, 'India revolves entirely within its own millenial creation. The Hindu writers of today work entirely within the traditions of their sacred literature. They are immersed in the past, in the Collective Unconscious of their race, and their writing is essentially a ritual. In this way, they are not just writers, but priests with a sacred charge.'

'And that is why Buddhism disappeared from India,' Hesse replied. 'It was too intellectual, and denied the world of symbols. . . . But to go back to Jung, I think he is quite right to interpret symbols. He is an immense mountain, an extraordinary genius. . . . I first met him through a mutual friend who was also interested in interpreting symbols, but I haven't seen him for years. When you next visit him, give him Steppenwolf's regards. . . .'

Hesse laughed merrily, and I then spoke:

'I asked Jung what he really thought the Self was, and he said that Western man considers Christ to be the Self.'

Immediately Hesse became serious. He remained silent and stared for a long time at the miniature painting which was resting against the wine bottle. Finally he looked at his wife and said, 'We ought to find something for our friend from Chile and India.'

Mrs. Hesse smiled and then she rose. 'I've already got something,' she said. She went over to one of the bookcases that lined the walls, and taking a small step ladder, climbed up to reach a book on an upper shelf. This she brought over to her husband, and then remained standing behind him, gently massaging the back of his head. I was then reminded that Mrs. Ceccarelli had told me that Hesse suffered from arthritis, and had warned me not to shake hands too firmly with him.

Hesse then handed me the book. It was a small volume written in his own handwriting, in Gothic script, and illustrated by his own watercolours. The book was called *Piktor's Metamorphosis*, and it was enclosed in a case which looked like an old Chinese box. Hesse then took the book and inscribed it on the first page: 'For our guest from Chile and India.'

We drank a glass of wine, and then Hesse led me into the dining-room to show me an oil painting of his native city, Calw. The painting showed a bridge arched across a river, and I imagined that it was there, while looking down on the waters below that Hesse first thought of Goldmund and Siddhartha, and considered the meaning of that river which, like the Ganges, swept everything before it to the sea.

Hesse then showed me a stone bust in another part of the room. It was a statue of his own head, carved by a friend of his who was a sculptress. He rested his hand on it, and I asked him:

'Is it important to know whether there is something beyond life?'

'No, it is not important. . . . The act of dying is like falling into Jung's Collective Unconscious, and from there you return to form, to pure form. . . .'

For a few moments Hesse remained silent, gently caressing the stone head.

Piktor's Metamorphosis

THAT NIGHT at Mr. Ceccarelli's inn I read the small book which Hesse had given me. This story, *Piktor's Metamorphosis* follows: Piktor had entered Paradise and found himself standing before a tree which represented both Man and Woman. He gazed at it with wonder and then asked, 'Are you the Tree of Life?' The tree made no reply, but instead the Serpent appeared, and so Piktor continued on his way. He examined everything with care and was delighted with what he saw.

As he walked along, he saw another tree which represented the Sun and the Moon. 'Perhaps you are the Tree of Life?' he asked. The Sun seemed to laugh in affirmation, and the Moon smiled. All about Piktor were clumps of wild flowers. They seemed to have faces like people, and some laughed richly and understandingly, while others swayed in a light-hearted manner. Still others neither moved nor laughed; they were sombre and sunk into themselves, as though drunk with their own perfume. Some of the flowers sang to Piktor: one sang him the wistful song of the lilacs, another a dark blue lullaby. One flower had eyes like hard sapphire; another reminded him of his first love; still another made him recall his mother's voice when he had wandered with her as a child in the gardens at home. Most of the flowers were gaily laughing, and one stuck out her tongue at him. It was a little pink tongue, and Piktor leaned down to touch it. When he did, he met the wild bitter taste of wine and honey, and he knew that it was the kiss of a woman.

Alone amongst all these flowers, Piktor was overwhelmed by a mixed feeling of nostalgia and fear. His heart was beating rapidly as though anxious to respond to the rhythms of the place. Piktor then saw a bird lying on the grass a little distance away. The bird had feathers like a peacock reflecting all the colours of the spectrum. Piktor was overwhelmed by the beauty of the bird, and so he approached and asked, 'Where can one find happiness?'

'Happiness?' replied the bird, 'Happiness is everywhere— in the mountains and the valleys and in every flower.'

The bird then stretched its neck and shook its feathers before settling back motionless. Suddenly Piktor realized that the bird had been transformed into a flower. The feathers had become leaves and the claws, roots. Piktor looked down in astonishment, and then almost immediately, the flower began to move its leaves. It had already grown tired of being a flower and began to float languidly up into the air. It had turned into a butterfly, and was a blaze of pure, floating colour.

To Piktor's increasing amazement, this happy bird-flower-butterfly flew about him in circles. After a while it glided to the earth like a snowflake and remained trembling by Piktor's feet. For a moment, its wings fluttered, and then suddenly it was transformed into a crystal radiating a deep red light. It glistened on the grass with fantastic brilliance.

As Piktor gazed down upon it, it seemed to be gradually disappearing into the ground, as though it were being drawn into the very centre of the earth. Just as it was about to vanish, Piktor reached down and grasped it. He held it tightly in his hand, because it seemed a talisman for every adventure in the world.

At that moment the Serpent slid down from a nearby tree and whispered into Piktor's ear, 'This jewel can turn you into anything you want to be. But tell it your wish quickly, before it disappears.' Afraid of losing the opportunity, Piktor whispered the secret word to the stone, and suddenly he was transformed into a tree. Piktor had always wanted to be a tree, because he admired their strength and serenity. Soon he felt his roots sink into the earth and his branches reach towards the sky. New leaves and branches sprouted from his trunk, and he was content. His thirsty roots absorbed the water from the earth, and his branches were cooled by the languid air of the forest. Insects lived in his bark, and a porcupine took shelter at his feet.

In the forest of Paradise in which he stood, he observed the continuing metamorphosis that took place round about him. He watched flowers become precious stones, or turn themselves into birds. He saw a neighbouring tree suddenly transform itself into a brook. Another became a crocodile, yet a third turned into a fish and swam off full of gaiety and happiness. All of creation took part in this game of change; elephants became rocks; giraffes, huge flowering trees.

In the midst of all this change, Piktor alone remained the same. When he began to realize his condition, he lost his happiness, and little by little he began to grow old, taking on that tired, absent look that one can observe in many old trees. Nor is this phenomenon confined to trees; horses and dogs and even human beings begin to disintegrate with time and to lose their beauty because they have lost the gift of metamorphosis. They end their days in sadness and worry.

A long time afterwards, a little girl with blonde hair lost her way while dancing through Paradise. She wore a blue dress and sang gaily as she skipped along. Her presence was eagerly noticed by other creatures in the forest; the bushes reached out towards her with their branches, and many trees threw down fruit for her. But the young girl ignored their attentions. At length she came into the little clearing where Piktor stood as a tree. When Piktor looked down at her, he was struck by a deep feeling of nostalgia and an immense desire to seize happiness before it was too late. He felt as though his whole being were commanding him to concentrate on the meaning of his existence and to force it to the surface of his consciousness. He recalled his past life, his years as a man before he entered Paradise. And he particularly remembered the time when he had held the magic jewel in his hands, because at that moment, with all changes possible, he had been most alive. He then recalled the bird and the gay tree which had represented the Sun and the Moon and as he did so he realized how fatal the Serpent's advice had been.

The girl sensed the restless movement of Piktor's leaves and branches, and when she looked up, she felt strangely disquieted. She sat in the shade, and intuitively began to understand that the tree was lonely and sad, while at the same time realizing that there was something noble in its total isolation. Leaning against the rough tree trunk, she sensed something of the turmoil that was going on in Piktor's being, and she too started to tremble in an inexplicable passion. Soon she was weeping, and as the tears fell on her dress, she wondered why it was that suffering existed. In her own solitude, she felt herself reaching out in compassion for the lonely tree.

Sensing her feelings, Piktor gathered all the forces of his life and directed them towards the young girl. He realised now how monstrous the Serpent's deception had been and how foolishly he had acted. Now as a single tree, he was overwhelmed with the vision of the tree that was man and woman together.

Just then, a green bird with red wings drew near and circled round the tree. The girl watched its flight and saw something bright and luminous fall from its beak into the nearby grass. She leaned over to pick it up and found that it was a precious carbuncle. She had hardly held the stone for a moment when the confused thoughts that had troubled her vanished, and she was overcome by a single desire. In a moment of ecstasy, she became one with the tree and was transformed into a new branch which grew out towards the heavens.

Now everything was perfect, and the world was in order. In that moment, Paradise had been found. Piktor was no longer a solitary old tree, but was fulfilled and complete and bore a new name which he called Piktoria. And thus he sang out, loud and clear, the word 'Piktoria!' And this phrase also signified 'Victoria' or Victory. At long last, he had been transformed, and he realized the truth of eternal metamorphosis, because he had been changed from a half to a whole.

From then on, he knew he would be able to transform himself as often as he liked. The force of continuing creation was now released within him, and he knew he could renew himself as a star or a fish or a cloud or a bird. But he also realized that whatever form he took would be a whole, and that in each image he would be a pair; he had both the Sun and the Moon within him, and he was at once Man and Woman.

That evening in Montagnola, when I finished reading the book and glanced once again at the drawings it contained, I thought of a phrase which Hesse himself had written only the year before: 'In their old age, some men have the gift of once again experiencing the paradisiacal state of their childhood.' That, I realized, was the key to the seemingly ingenuous tale of Piktor. It was really a vision of Paradise regained. And then too, there came back upon me with redoubled force Hermann Hesse's remark of the afternoon before when, with his hand on the stone bust, he had said, 'We will return to form, to pure form. . . .'

Morning

THE NEXT MORNING I got up early and went out into the garden to watch the sun rise over Lake Lugano. Afterwards I wandered slowly through the narrow streets of the town until once again I found myself at Hesse's house. By this time, the sun was full up, but I was surprised to find Hesse in the garden standing by the fence and wearing a broad-brimmed hat. He was burning grass. He then noticed me and went to open the gate.

We exchanged greetings, and I then showed him that I was carrying *Piktor's Metamorphosis*. He took the volume, and together we looked at the drawings once again. I told him how wonderful I thought they were, and he laughed gaily. 'They are crystals, birds, butterflies—everything for just a second, as in Creation.'

'And Piktor?' I asked.

'Piktor contains them all; he is all that and something else besides. . . .'

'You mean that he is Siddhartha's river,' I asked, 'the eternal river of forms, of Maya?'

'And also Steppenwolf,' Hesse replied. 'Some people can't understand that I could have written both *Siddhartha* and *Steppenwolf*. But they complement each other; they are the two poles of life between which we move. . . .'

Hesse paused and glanced again at the *Metamorphosis*. Then, as if talking to himself, he said, 'Yesterday when you visited me, it was my son's birthday. He was fifty years old. . . .'

I took my leave and walked downhill away from the house. When I found an open clearing in the trees, I lay down in the dry grass. I pushed my hands through it, as if looking for the stone of metamorphosis, but I didn't find it.

Later on, I returned by the same road and saw that Hesse was still in his garden burning grass. Enveloped in smoke, he looked like someone performing an ancient rite. Someone then came down the garden path whom I soon recognized as Hesse's wife. She was carrying a basket over her shoulder, and as she approached, she coquettishly smoothed back her grey hair. I realized that this gesture was intended to please Hesse and I was almost ashamed at having witnessed it. It was touching to think that that mature woman wanted to look beautiful for an eighty-year-old man, and it was an indication of the profundity of their relationship. I decided to leave, but as I walked away, I could still see them as they went along the garden paths. She went in front and he behind, picking weeds to place in the basket. I imagined that that was how the wise Chinese of antiquity must have lived. In reality, Hesse seemed like an old Chinese philosopher or like the wise tree of his story. When I passed by the house, he saw me again. He turned and took off his wide-brimmed hat to wave good-bye.

Master Djü-dschi

TWO YEARS LATER, I returned to Montagnola to bring Hesse one of the first copies of *The Visits of the Queen of Sheba*, a book which I had written in India. It was a Sunday, January 22, 1961, and the town was now covered with snow. As usual, I first went to the old house where Hesse used to live, and I noticed that the old plane trees were sheathed in white.

Later on, I walked slowly up the hill towards Hesse's present house. The walking was difficult, and when I heard the sound of an automobile engine, I moved to the side of the road to let it pass. As it drew near, the car stopped, however, and a hand waved at me through the frosted windows. It was Hesse, and his wife was driving. I got in and we continued along the way.

'We've just come from the city,' Hesse said; 'I went to buy this for you.' He then handed me a copy of *Neue Zürcher Zeitung*. It contained a poem of his which had been published in the Sunday Supplement.

'I will use this poem to answer all the questions you may put to me today,' he said.

Almost immediately we reached the house, and soon we were in the familiar living-room. Hesse and I sat down and I noticed that he looked a little thinner than he had two years before. I then took up the newspaper and read the poem.

THE RAISED FINGER

Master Djü-dschi was, so we are informed,
Of a quiet and gentle disposition, and so modest
That he renounced totally both word and doctrine,
For word is appearance, and he was scrupulously anxious
To shun every appearance.

When students, monks and novices
Engaged in noble speech and in intellectual fireworks
Concerning the meaning of the world and the highest
Good, he kept silent watch,
On guard against every effusion.

And when they came to him with their questions,
The vain as well as the serious, concerning the meaning
Of the ancient scriptures, concerning the names of the Buddha,
Concerning illumination, concerning the beginning of the world
And its destruction, he remained silent,
Only pointing quietly upward with his finger.

And this finger's mutely-eloquent pointing
Became always more fervent and more admonishing; it spoke,
It taught, praised, punished, pierced so peculiarly
Into the heart of the world and truth, that with time,
More than one disciple understood this gentle raising of the finger,
Trembled, and woke up.

When I finished the poem, I glanced over at Hesse and saw
him raise his finger. For a while, we sat quietly together,
watching the snowflakes slowly falling outside of the window.
Finally he broke the silence:

'Words are really a mask,' he said. 'They rarely express the
true meaning; in fact they tend to hide it. If you can live in
fantasy, then you don't need religion, since with fantasy you
can understand that after death, man is reincorporated in the
Universe. Once again I will say that it is not important to
know whether there is something beyond this life. What counts
is having done the right sort of work; if that is right, then
everything else will be all right. The Universe, or Nature, is
for me what God is for others. It is wrong to think that Nature
is the enemy of man, something to be conquered. Rather,
we should look upon Nature as a mother, and should peaceably
surrender ourselves to it. If we take that attitude, we will
simply feel that we are returning to the Universe as all other
things do, all animals and all plants. We are all just infinites-
imal parts of the Whole. It is absurd to rebel; we must deliver
ourselves up to the great current. . . .'

'And what about the individual *persona*?' I asked. 'It always
resists and rebels. In the Orient, of course, individuality doesn't

3. Title page of Hesse's *Piktor's Metamorphosis*, inscribed to the author.

4. One of Hesse's illustrations for *Piktor's Metamorphosis*.

exist as it does in Christian countries. Indeed, the *persona* seems to be a product of Christianity, just the way love is, since love is a by-product of the *persona*. Without personality, there can be no love, or at least no love that is truly passionate.'

Since Hesse seemed to agree with my analysis, I continued:

'In the same way, beauty, or at least the concept of individualized beauty, is a product of the *persona*. This is as true of the beauty of gesture, or of the beauty of a personal life as it is of the beauty of streets or squares or cathedrals in the cities of Europe. Nature of course is beautiful, but in a quite different fashion. This is best seen when one considers the temples and monuments of the Orient. They are beautiful only in the way a waterfall or a forest can be beautiful—in a wholly impersonal manner. I have known Swamis who were completely indifferent to the beauty of Florence. The idea of the *persona* has not yet reached the Orient, and the personal isn't understood, any more than love is, in the Western Christian sense. That is not a criticism; it is simply a statement of fact. Indeed, for the West, the idea of the *persona* may be the source of our sickness, may be the very curse of our existence. . . .'

I paused for a moment and thought about what Hesse had said to me concerning his book, *Siddhartha*, and especially the twenty years that had passed between its original publication and its appearance in India. Even today, many orthodox Hindus consider this book to be a false re-working of Oriental truth from a Christian point of view. *Siddhartha* is the drama of an individualized soul, and the conscious acts which Siddhartha performs throughout the latter part of his life are the results of the continuing presence of reason.

'It is strange,' I said, 'to see how the Hindus continue to revolve round their Vedas and their Bhagavad Gita. They never create anything new, and even the abstract painters of modern India end up by reinterpreting the Ramayana.'

'But surely that is a good thing,' said Hesse. 'That is the whole strength of Hinduism. It follows a single line; it is interested in concentration and opposed to dispersion. Don't forget, one must beware of taking on too much. . . . Moreover, you must remember that if the Hindus read little, it's because the English didn't allow translations of European thought to

reach them. I think at heart you are really trying to defend the
West, and that is probably because the West is losing today
and the Orient is rising once again.'

'No,' I said, 'that's not it at all. I don't feel any more sympathy for the West than I do for the East. I don't belong to
either one, because as a South American I find myself caught
between the two.'

Hesse raised his finger like Master Djü-dschi, and said,
'Don't forget that words are masks. . . .'

Just then Mrs. Hesse came in and asked us to go into the
dining-room. It was full of light, and the picture of Calw,
Hesse's birthplace, hung on the wall. Mrs. Elsy Bodmer, the
widow of the owner of the house who had been Hesse's friend,
was the other guest invited. Hesse then told us that lunch
would be served in the Hindu fashion.

'When I was a child in Calw,' he said, 'we always had curry
on Sundays, and we would have children from the colonies
come to lunch with us. Both my grandfather and father knew
India intimately, and from them I learned to love the god
Krishna.'

We had red wine from Ticino, and Hesse and I drank a
toast together. The bright daylight played on the crystal of
the glasses, causing spectra of colour to fall on the tablecloth.
Hesse sat at the other end of the table and, with his glass still
in his hand, he looked as though he were meditating, and the
white light which reflected from the table seemed to increase
the blueness of his eyes.

'How is it that I am here?' I asked, uttering the words slowly
and heavily. 'How is it that I have come from so far away,
and have had the luck to find myself here with you today?'

Hesse remained still, bathed in the winter light, and then
he spoke: 'Nothing ever happens by chance,' he said, 'here only
the right guests meet. This is the Hermetic Circle. . . .'

I then realized that those words were by no means casual,
but that they had emerged from a purely symbolic realm.
Now at last I felt that Hesse was giving some meaning to my
wanderings and travels, talking to me as Siddhartha had once
spoken to Govinda. I remained silent, and as I looked at him,
I had the feeling that the Master Djü-dschi was again repeating
his gesture. . . .

A Letter

WHEN I RETURNED to India, I wrote the following letter to Hesse:

'I want to thank you for that Sunday with you, and for the privilege of belonging to the Hermetic Circle, which is like being a member of the League in your *Journey to the East*. In fact, I felt as though I really were a member of that timeless League, and when I was in Küsnacht, I told Dr. Jung what you had said about the "right guests". . . . In any event, I am trying to continue this journey across connecting bridges. The other day, the *I Ching* revealed that that was my destiny. In my case, the bridges connect South America, Europe and Asia.

'When I returned here, I reread your poem about Master Djü-dschi, and I believe that I understand its meaning. You said that words were a mask, and that is true; but it is also true that underneath the dialogue of words, there is another dialogue, and it is this second one to which we must listen, since it is the only one which really matters. It is the basis for the celebration at Bremgarten.[1]

'I gave Steppenwolf's regards to Professor Jung. He smiled and asked about you. We talked about many things, and I learned that he also knows how to make the gesture of Master Djü-dschi. . . .'

The Last Meeting

HESSE'S BOOK *The Journey to the East* is the story of a celebration which the author offers to his own being, as well as to the characters he has created in his books and to the myths which have affected him. This celebration, or festival, takes place half-way through his life, in the course of a search, or journey to the East, in which he finds himself a member of a League of pilgrims. This search begins in and extends through mountains and valleys; it is possible that these represent the Alps, but it is more likely that they form the interior landscape of the

[1] Reference to a spiritual meeting in Hesse's book, *The Journey to the East*.

author's soul. The East is always the country of the soul and the source of light. The pilgrims were all looking for impossible things: one was trying to find the Serpent Kundalini; Hesse was searching for the Princess Fatima. Amongst the pilgrims, there was one who was called Leo, the Server, who always helped the others. The great symbolic celebration takes place in Bremgarten in magnificent surroundings. Everyone is there—Don Quixote, Hölderlin, who was greatly admired by Hesse, Hoffman and Henry of Ofterdingen. In addition, all of Hesse's characters are also present: Steppenwolf, Demian, Paul the musician, Klingsor the painter, Narcissus, Goldmund, Siddhartha and Govinda, in all of whom Hesse had been reincarnated during his lifetime.

But then something tragic happens. Leo, the Server, is lost, or has abandoned them, and so the journey to the East is interrupted. All the friends disperse, and the League is broken. One wonders who this Leo is, who, by simply disappearing, can produce such a catastrophe. It was not until much later in his life that Hesse was able to find him. He would seem to reappear in his work as Joseph Knecht, the great teacher in *Magister Ludi*, a book which he dedicated to the pilgrims to the East. Knecht means 'server' in German.

The Journey to the East ends with a strange symbol, the author's encounter with a figurine in the archives of the League. This little statuette is finally revealed as being hermaphroditic or androgynous, but before that revelation takes place, Hesse has had to pass many tests, amongst them one concerning the Alsatian dog, Necker, and another meeting with Leo, the Server. Of all Hesse's works, *The Journey to the East* is the most hermetic. I have never tried to interpret it, but have simply allowed myself to sink into its subtle beauty.

It was Saturday, May 6, 1961. I had not let much time pass before visiting Hesse again, and I had brought with me a little silver box from Kashmir, which was embossed with turquoises. I had brought another one like it for Professor Jung.

'I have just come from Florence,' I said; 'I went there just to see Leonardo's painting of "The Annunciation" in the Uffizi Gallery. I stayed there almost an hour looking at it.'

'Why were you so especially interested in that painting?' he asked.

'It's difficult, but I will try to explain. In Leonardo there is a *something*, a message that can only be perceived, not interpreted, just as in *The Journey to the East*. The painting of "The Annunciation" seems literally to vibrate. The angel's wings flutter in the air, and the fingers of his right hand as he makes the sign really seem to be alive. Something seems to be transmitted from those fingers to the young Virgin, but the really searing message comes from the eyes. It's as though this terrible angel were actually delivering Christ to the Virgin with his look, as though he were actually impregnating her with him. She is frightened and childish, and receives the message with her left hand while her right rests on the books of the Prophets. That is why she says, "*It was written*," but I dare say Leonardo put that in only to please the Curia. The truth is that the Virgin is so surprised that she accepts everything; in fact she has been hypnotized, possessed by the angel, and she will never be herself again. In the background of the painting there is that dreamlike landscape so typical of Leonardo, which seems to represent the Unconscious, from which everything comes—mystery, destiny, Christ and the very angel that appears in the painting.'

Hesse had listened attentively while I spoke, and after a pause, he said, 'Leonardo was a universal genius because his painting was magical. Most people only understand what they feel with their senses; they know nothing of what lies behind them. Only magic can express that which is unreachable in any other way. There is also another kind of art, which is essentially evocative.'

'*Demian* and *The Journey to the East* exist in that magical realm, I suppose. . . . But who, by the way, is Leo?'

For a moment, Hesse glanced away and watched a cat enter through the open window. He ran his hand over the back of the cat, and then said: 'Leo is someone who is able to converse with animals, with the dog, Necker, for example. . . . A friend of mine once had a dog which he had to give away. He took the dog fifty kilometres away and left him there. But the dog escaped and returned; he found the road. . . . That too is magical. . . .'

'Who do you think most resembles Leonardo in music?' I then asked. 'Who is the magic musician?'

'Bach,' said Hesse without hesitation. 'Especially in his Mass and in the Passions according to St. Matthew and St. John. These are the magical works, and I always used to go into Zurich when these works were being performed there.'

Hesse then rose and walked slowly over to the bookcase.

'Have you written anything since the *Magister Ludi*?' I asked.

'Evocations,' he replied, as though he had not been listening. 'The poet has to evoke the past and to relive it, to seize the ephemeral. That is an important part of his work.'

Hesse then showed me an Italian translation of one of his works.

'The Italians have at last begun to translate me,' he said. 'And to think that I live in the Italian part of Switzerland! It's quite different in Spain. You know that the publisher Aguilar has already begun to publish my complete works. You must look at them and tell me whether you think they are accurate. You know, of course, that in Germany there is now a great interest in Spanish and South American authors.' He then showed me a German edition of a book by the Venezuelan writer Romulo Gallegos.

Before I left him that afternoon, we talked about a number of writers, and I asked him whether he had known Rilke.

'I didn't know him,' he replied. 'But speaking of translations, I think that Rilke is better understood in translation than he is in the original.'

'And Keyserling, did you know him?'

'Yes, he was an extraordinary man; an immense and powerful being capable of roaring like a bull.' And Hesse then tried to imitate Keyserling's bellow.

'And Gustav Meyrink, what was he like?'

'I knew Meyrink well. He was seriously interested in magic and he practiced it. When he was in great danger, he would concentrate on his heart and maintain an inalterable calm. At the same time, he had a sharp sense of humour. Once, right in the middle of a seance, just when the visitor from the beyond was supposed to appear, Meyrink lit a match so that he could see him, and that of course was the end of the seance. He was also fascinated by black magic.'

When I left that afternoon, Mrs. Hesse invited me for lunch on the following day.

Sunday, May 7, 1961

I ARRIVED FAIRLY EARLY, and we resumed our conversation of the afternoon before. I mentioned Arthur Koestler's recent book on India and Japan called *The Lotus and the Robot*. 'He attacks Suzuki very harshly in that book,' I said.

'You can be sure that Suzuki won't lose sleep over that,' Hesse replied. 'He doesn't allow himself to be touched. . . .'

As I heard Hesse's words, I remembered a story that is told about Jesus. He was going through the streets of Jerusalem on his way to cure a sick woman when he suddenly stopped and exclaimed, 'Who has touched my cloak and taken away my power to cure?'

I told Hesse that I had been with Koestler when he was in India looking for material for his book. I had asked him for dinner in my house in New Delhi, and afterwards we went to see a Sufi mystic called Sister Raihana. She was able to discover the past of people's lives by reading the backs of their hands, not their palms. I didn't tell her who Koestler was, and so she simply took his hand, concentrated for a moment and then told him that in his previous incarnation, he had been an Army chaplain.

Hesse then asked me whether I myself was writing anything at the moment, and I said that for the past five years I had been writing a book about my experiences in India, which was a kind of search between two worlds.

'What are you going to call it?' he asked.

'The title finally came to me while I was looking at the ruins of Angkor in Cambodia,' I said. 'You know that the causeway which leads up to the great temple of Angkor Wat is bordered on either side by a balustrade carved in the shape of stone serpents. When I looked at them, I thought of the Serpent Kundalini which leads one along the path to liberation; and I remembered that the serpent is curled at the base of the spinal column and that it in turn represents the Tree of Paradise. Since my book deals with the Serpent and the Tree,

I have decided to call it *The Serpent of Paradise*. It is after all a symbolic and subjective journey like your own to the East, and I have always been particularly interested in Yoga and in the science which deals with Kundalini.'

Hesse then said that he thought Kundalini really represented knowledge. He added that he thought Yoga was essentially a means whereby the animal could be raised to a higher plane, not consciously but in an almost alchemical fashion.

I then asked him whether he had ever practiced Yoga.

'Only the Yoga of breathing,' he replied, 'but that was some time ago, and I used Chinese rather than Indian methods. In the West, I think it is not only difficult but dangerous to practice Yoga, because the atmosphere isn't appropriate for exercises which require complete solitude. Here we are too much impinged upon by the actualities of ordinary life. Real Yoga can only be practiced in India.'

I was puzzled by what Hesse had said, for in Montagnola, he had achieved almost complete isolation in the mountains. And I myself had practiced concentration in the Andes, and even in hotels and in busy city streets.

'But isn't the mind like a radio,' I asked, 'which is able to transmit and receive wherever it is, on mountain tops or in crowded places? Surely there is a kind of collective mind which receives the emanations from an individual mind wherever it is located. At times I don't even believe that physical action or personal contact is necessary to achieve results. You know that in Banaras, there is a handful of solitary Brahmans who practice concentration, repeating magic formulas and ancient *mantrams* in order to maintain peace in the world. Perhaps they accomplish more than the United Nations does. Yes, I think the mind is like a radio. . . .'

'Everything is much more complicated and subtle than that,' Hesse replied. 'The kind of attitude you speak of can only exist in India, which is prepared and ready for it. In Europe, it is perhaps possible in a few Catholic convents; I don't know, but I myself am on another track. . . .'

'In the Benedictine convents?' I asked.

Hesse nodded his head affirmatively.

'And what do you think will happen in the future,' I asked, 'with the new interest in spaceships, Sputniks, and interplanetary journeys? Do you think man will continue to be concerned with problems of the spirit?'

'Ah!' Hesse exclaimed, 'in fifty years the earth will be a graveyard of machines, and the soul of the spaceman will simply be the cabin of his own rocket!'

Lunch was then served, and we went into the dining-room. One of the guests was the daughter of Hugo Ball, Hesse's first biographer and the author of *Byzantine Christianity*. Hesse had also carried on a long and interesting correspondence with the guest's mother, and it had been published in a handsome volume.

Once again I looked at the painting of the little city of Calw with its old bridge, and I decided that one day I would have to visit that German city about which Hesse had written so beautifully.

Hesse seemed more and more to be returned to the emotions of his early years, and once again I wondered how it was that a chosen few were able, in their most advanced years, to relive the feelings they had experienced near Paradise in their infancy.

Hesse sat at the far end of the table, not far from his own stone bust. His smile was like that of an ancient child who had returned to Paradise, after a long struggle for his soul, a struggle which he had won through his constant fidelity to Nature. He raised a glass full of red wine from the Ticino and said in Spanish, 'Salud'.

That is my last image of Hermann Hesse.

Last Messages

AFTER THAT MEETING with Hesse, I went to Küsnacht to see Professor Jung. He was then very ill, and it proved to be my last visit with him as well, since I received news of his death when I returned to New Delhi. At that time I wrote Hermann Hesse to tell him about my last meeting with Jung, and after describing how he had then appeared, I added the following paragraphs:

'And now here I am once again thinking about Dr. Jung. I wonder whether there is something in the Hermetic Circle which suggests that we had all known one another in other lives? Why else have you both been so congenial to me? If we knew one another before, does it mean that we shall meet again? And if so, when and where?

'I sit here thinking about that great figure, Dr. Jung, and about yourself. But mostly, I think about the relationship which existed between him, you, and me. Each time I visited you, I always went to see him as well. A short time ago, I took your greetings to him.'

On July 29, 1961, the Swiss newspaper *Neue Zürcher Zeitung* published a special supplement in honour of Dr. Jung. I myself sent an article entitled 'My Last Meeting with Dr. Jung' which was later to be published in various Spanish magazines and in an English translation in India. When I received the special supplement after it was published, I was astonished to find on the same page with my article, the letter which I had written to Hermann Hesse.

A few days later, I received a letter from him:

'With Jung I have also lost something irreplaceable. And only recently, the oldest of my friends, the artist Cuno Amiet died at the age of ninety-four years. Now I have only friends who are younger than myself.

'I must now confess something to you: I knew that the *Zürcher Zeitung* was preparing a page in memory of Jung. I myself was unable to contribute anything because I was not well. Nevertheless I took the liberty of sending your letter to me, the one you wrote me after Jung's death, to the newspaper, and I will take the responsibility for it. I hope that you won't mind.'

Yours,
Hermann Hesse.

My Departure from India

AFTER LIVING IN INDIA for nearly ten years, I decided that the time had come to leave. I had submerged myself in that Dionysiac culture and world; and I had touched its essences with both hands, dissolving myself in that strange atmosphere in which time is a cosmic river, sweeping before it the debris of actual life, including the *persona* itself, that delicate flower of Christianity and the extroverted West.

Nevertheless, even though I had plumbed the depths of Indian life, and had lived like a Hindu, I realized that I really was not a part of Indian culture. At the same time, I knew that I was not a Westerner either. Rather, I was caught between two worlds. That is, of course, the continuing drama of the South American, who is able to participate in both universes, but only in a relative way, and who is therefore forced to try to discover his own separate identity.

Soon word came that my government had appointed me as its Ambassador to Yugoslavia. Chile has long maintained a tradition which favours writers in the diplomatic corps; it is its way of encouraging searchers and pilgrims. When I received that news, I wrote to Hermann Hesse and said, 'Now I shall be nearer to you physically.'

Nearer? Even then Hesse was on the way to his end.

Before I settled in Belgrade, I went to Spain. There I looked for the Aguilar edition of Hesse's complete works so that I could tell him about the translation. I was travelling with my eldest son, and he was most anxious to meet Hesse. At that time, however, we were in a hurry. and although we drove by the Lago di Garda, in Italy, which is not far from Montagnola, we were unable to stop. And then something happened which prevented my son's wish from being fulfilled.

I was standing at a newspaper kiosk in Belgrade, looking for a newspaper written in a language which I could understand. At last, I found an old copy of the London *Times*. And there, together with a photograph, was the news of Hermann Hesse's death.

I went straight home from the kiosk, and all that day and the following day I remained there, meditating and concentrating my thoughts on my dead friend.

Not long afterwards, since my son had to leave Europe, I went with him to Zürich, and together we made a last pilgrimage to Montagnola to visit Hesse's widow and to express our sympathy to her.

Once again, and perhaps for the last time, I was in Montagnola. The Albergo Bellavista and Signor Ceccarelli were the same as before. I showed my son the old house in the town, and from there we went to where Hesse had lived until his death. We waited in the parlour until Ninon Hesse appeared. She was dressed in black, and her whole being seemed to be concentrated in her face. She was as beautiful as before but appeared to be marked by destruction. The many years she had spent in the study of art, music and nature, all in Hesse's company, had come to an end.

We sat down together and remained silent for a long time. At length she spoke:

'When you came here for the first time some years ago, I had been stung by a bee and so was not with you when you talked to Hesse. But afterwards he told me about you. "Today somebody came whom I seem to know, and whom I think to be my friend—a young man from Chile," he said. Hesse liked you, and a good relationship existed between you. . . .'

'You don't know how much I regret not having come a week earlier,' I said. 'My son wanted so much to meet Hermann Hesse. . . .'

'He died very suddenly, and that was for the best. He was very ill. He had suffered from leukemia for six years, but did not know that he had it. Nevertheless, sometimes when he felt exalted before nature, standing in the twilight or in the moonlight, he sensed that he was saying good-bye to life. He had a presentiment that he was nearing the end. He had been working for several days on a poem, and only finished it on the night of his death. He left it for me on my bed, and I found it there. Afterwards, when I went into his room at dawn, he was dead. He had died in his sleep. His poem was about an old tree, and he wondered whether he would be there to see it again next year. . . .'

Ninon Hesse then gave me a copy of the poem.

A few moments later, Mrs. Elsy Bodmer came into the room. She had come over to keep Mrs. Hesse company during the day. Without saying a word, she sat down beside her. Just then, the cat passed through the window, and Mrs. Hesse looked at it penetratingly.

'It has been looking for Hermann all through the house,' she said. 'It looks for him all day and all night. Somehow it seems to feel, as I do, his presence. . . . But I must tell you about something quite beautiful which happened. By chance, or perhaps not by chance, Hesse's childhood friend, the clergyman Voelter, happened to be spending his vacation in the Sels Engadin when Hesse died. They used to argue at great length about Luther, for whom Hermann had no great love. Voelter came over to Montagnola for Hermann's burial and delivered a sermon over his grave. It was an impressive sight to watch that tall, thin figure carrying out a ritual for which he seemed predestined to perform because of his long friendship with Hermann.'

Ninon Hesse then glanced towards the bookshelves and pointed out a coloured drawing of a bird flying up towards the heavens.

'That drawing was sent to Hermann Hesse for his birthday, only a few weeks before he died,' she said. 'He was happy with it and spent a long time looking at it. He was really a bird himself.'

I then remembered *Demian* and the drawing of Sinclair's bird with the legend under it: 'The egg is the World, and the bird breaks the shell; afterwards it flies towards God, and God is called Abraxas.'

That afternoon my son and I went to see the cemetery in Montagnola where Hesse was buried. His name had not yet been carved on the stone, and only a few yellow flowers covered the earth. My son left me there for a long time, and I sat on the grass across from the grave and thought of my friend, that master poet, trying to recall his features, and to fix them in my mind as they had been before he had been carried down that immense river which vanishes completely in the sea and which disperses everything beyond the recall of memory. And then I remembered his words: 'To die is to go into the Collective Unconscious, to lose oneself in order to be transformed into form, pure form.'

I then heard someone coming along the path and, looking up, saw a young couple. They carried knapsacks and wore shorts and hob-nailed boots. They were talking in German, and when they reached me, they asked whether that was Hesse's grave. I told them that it was, and they stood there together in an attitude of profound introspection, the girl with her head on the young man's shoulder. They remained there for some time until at last, the young man opened his knapsack and took out a little book bound in light blue. He then began to read a poem by the dead writer. As though they were praying, those young Germans read his own verses to Hesse. I wondered whether he would hear them in some ray of as yet uncreated light which existed apart from the waters that were now carrying him away.

The Tree

THAT NIGHT my son and I read Hesse's last poem:

THE RUSTLING OF A BROKEN BRANCH

> The broken, splintered branch
> hanging year after year,
> dryly rattles its song in the wind;
> without foliage, without bark,
> it is barren and faded.
> Tired of living too long,
> tired of dying too long,
> its song is hard and tenacious;
> it sounds arrogant, hiding the fear.
>
> One more summer.
> Another long winter.

Goldmund's Statue

AFTER MY SON'S DEPARTURE, I stayed on alone in Zürich for a number of days. One of the people I wanted to see was Mrs. Elsy Bodmer, and I had to wait for her return from Montagnola before calling on her.

The Bodmer house is one of the oldest in Zürich, dating from the end of the sixteenth century. To cross the threshold of that house is to leave the modern world. Mrs. Bodmer keeps the house as it always was; even the rooms in which her children were born are maintained as they were when they lived in them, with their furniture and their toys. The beams in the main rooms are noble and ancient, and the walls are covered with paintings by Botticelli and medieval wood carvings.

I climbed up to the top floor where Elsy Bodmer received me in an airy salon. Hesse had been there on many occasions to see his friend, Hans Bodmer. After greeting me, Mrs. Bodmer began to talk about Hesse. 'There was an important link between you and him,' she said, 'In his last years he had no new friends, and saw no one. But with you it was different. . . . It is odd, your coming from so far away and being so much younger than him. . . .' She then fell silent as though meditating.

'Do you think Mrs. Hesse will remain in Montagnola?' I said.

'I imagine so. I asked my son whether he wanted to live in the Montagnola house, but he wants to leave it to Mrs. Hesse. It all depends on whether she can get used to the loneliness.'

'Are there any plans for a Hesse museum, containing his books and manuscripts?'

'Yes, but they haven't decided where. Some people think it ought to be in Berne; others in Germany. It seems to me that Berne is a little isolated, just as Lugano would be. What do you think?'

'I think that the time has now come for Hermann Hesse to return from his exile to Germany.' As I spoke, I had the feeling that Hesse was urging me on, and I remembered also the young German couple who had stood next to his grave.

Elsy Bodmer then said, 'I believe you are right. There is also some indication that Hesse wanted that too. He was once asked about it, and he mentioned the German city which contains the Rilke museum.'

'Yes,' I said, 'and after all Hermann Hesse was profoundly German—the last in the romantic line of Hölderlin. He was also very German with his interest in the Orient, and especially

India. He was just like Schopenhauer and Nietzsche in that respect. Moreover, I think that the time has come for Germany to repay its debt to Hesse. He has written so movingly about the old cities and roads of Germany—Nürnberg and his own little village of Calw.' I then told Mrs. Bodmer the story of the young German couple whom I had met at Montagnola.

'I'll tell Mrs. Hesse about that,' she said. 'And I will also tell her your opinion so that she can decide where the museum should be built.[1] By the way, have you ever seen the Thomas Mann museum here in Zürich? It's very interesting.'

'No,' I said, 'I didn't know it was here. I thought Mann had returned permanently to Germany.'

'You know that Mann completely condemned Germany during the last war, and the Germans never forgave him for it. They let him know what they thought about him when he revisited Germany after the war. Hesse also left Germany, but he never condemned it the way Mann did.'

I then said that I thought Mann's total condemnation of Germany showed that he was German to the core. Germany is very like Spain, I added, very absolutist; and that was why Mann had been carried away, and had lost a sense of proportion.

Mrs. Bodmer then offered me some old wine in a beautiful crystal goblet. A few moments later I rose to leave, but Mrs. Bodmer then said she wanted to show me some Renaissance paintings and an icon which were in another room. As we passed through the hall, I noticed a statue which immediately fascinated me. It was a life-sized carving of a monk, and Mrs. Bodmer told me that it was made in the twelfth century.

I stood before this extraordinary figure for some time. The young monk was depicted with his head shaved and his feet bare, wearing only a loose shawl. In his left hand he held some small tablets, and his right hand made the sign of the benediction. The hands and feet were very beautiful and the whole figure seemed extraordinarily fragile and delicate. The eyes seemed to look out from a remote epoch in time, from

[1] The Hermann Hesse archives have been donated to the Swiss Government who have agreed to lend them to the Hermann Hesse Museum which will be set up in part of the Schiller National Museum in Marbach in Germany.

5. One of Hesse's illustrations for *Piktor's Metamorphosis*.

6. One of Hesse's illustrations for *Piktor's Metamorphosis*.

the very dawn of Christianity if not indeed from an earlier, less differentiated period.

Hesse's hero, Goldmund, who was a vagabond along the roads of medieval Europe, created only one work of art in his life, and that was a wooden sculpture for the pulpit of a church. I imagined that, like this statue, it was the product of an entire life, and that it must have contained all the light and shadow of a life.

The Dream

THAT NIGHT IN ZÜRICH I had a dream. I saw a large white building several storeys high which looked like a University. It was full of students, most of them were studying the exact or applied sciences, engineering or physics. They all seemed to be using their knowledge to achieve tangible results; they were applying it automatically without a thought to the significance of what they were doing. They were untroubled by doubt and had no concern for vital essences. This University of my dream seemed to represent the world of the future. The men coming out of the class-rooms were hard and metallic, expressing themselves only in the laws of mechanics, and were themselves becoming products of those laws. The last exponents of a world of flesh and blood had departed and, with their concern for a living earth with gods and demons, were considered by this new generation of anti-men as romantic idealists, the product merely of a decayed bourgeois society. Thus my dream seemed to suggest that the archetype of the future—or indeed of the present since that future has already arrived—would be the man of the atom and the machine, preparing himself for the conquest of space in a University building made entirely of concrete and surrounded by asphalt.

In such a world I would be a total alien, unable to find a single niche for myself. But I then realized that people like Hesse and Jung had faced similar difficulties. They had now departed and were now untouched by the mechaniation of the earth and they had achieved other worlds which they had earned through realizing their own beings. I had little time left, but I knew that I myself would now have to make a similar effort so that I would never again return to this earth, but would step into another sphere. This I had to do if I was to save myself from the leaden desert into which the world was being transformed by machines. To escape from that horrible prison, I had to move along the same solitary path that had been followed by my older comrades, those wise men of flesh and blood who were the keepers of my dreams.

The Bremgarten Festival

IT WAS A SUNDAY, and I was alone in my house in Belgrade, surrounded by my Oriental paintings and sculptures. I decided that I would celebrate a ritual and listen to the magic music that Hesse had loved, Bach's Mass in B Minor. I lit a few sandalwood sticks and placed the records on the gramophone.

The point of my ritual was to listen to the music with Hesse, to lend him my senses, so that he could hear it, and make his presence felt. I leaned back on the sofa and let the music play over both of us. I did not concentrate on any of the notes in particular, for I knew he was listening through me, and I wanted him to listen as he had done when he was alive. As the sounds filled the room, I knew that they were the musical equivalents of Leonardo's painting of the Annunciation and of the Passion of St. John, for in that Mass, Bach was reliving his whole life, offering his symbols and legends to something which transcended him. It was a Mass with himself; it was a sacrifice to his own life and soul, a continuing search for the final marriage which is celebrated by an almost sacrilegious offering. It was about death and resurrection, but in its incorporation of Bach's own myths and rhythms, expressed through the interplay of notes in counterpoint, the music produced a symbolic Flower, which in turn was the product of the sustained tension of a soul that had cried from the cradle to the grave: 'Father, why has thou forsaken me?' That was the magic, the creation of a Mystical Flower. Few had achieved it. Bach had done so in his Mass, but the Mass was also a festival of Bremgarten, which Bach had offered to himself, repeating it throughout his entire creative life.

I continued to listen, missing nothing, and I knew that

Hesse was there and that he was grateful for it. He was also teaching me to listen as he had done. The Mass ended, and was followed by the Passions of St. John and St. Matthew. The whole day passed in the celebration of this ritual, and was my own Festival of Bremgarten.

I then decided to prepare a luncheon in my solitary house in Belgrade. It was to be in honour of the dear departed, and I was repaying the hospitality of Montagnola. But I also invited all my phantoms and legends. I led them into the dining-room and seated them at the table, while the magic music continued to play. At the table we were grouped in the form of a *mandala*.

At first, I had intended the party to be in honour of Hesse, but little by little it turned into a Mass performed in my own soul with the dreams of a lifetime. Then I served red wine from Istria and from the Andes. I drank a toast to Hesse to ease his road beyond the grave. I also promised that I would keep him in my memory, and I drank a toast to each one of my phantoms and for the great world of dreams.

We drank many toasts while the magical choristers continued to sing, and we felt enfolded in them, and in the very essence of a Legend beyond time or space.

Extracts from Two Letters

Belgrade,
October 6, 1962

Dear Mrs. Hesse,

When I was in Zürich I bought Bach's B Minor Mass and the Passions according to St. Matthew and St. John, and I listened to them here in Belgrade. I had the extraordinary feeling that Hermann Hesse was listening as well. I lent him my ears so that he could enjoy the sound of these great works.

Dear Mrs. Hesse, you must do the same; lend him your senses, and live happily for a long time so that he can continue to live through you. This is a ritual which we must perform for all our dear friends—for these who have already departed for the other shores. . . .

Yours devoutly,
Miguel Serrano

October 21, 1962

Dear Mr. Serrano,

... I am sure that Hermann Hesse would have been happy to know that you had brought the Bach records, the B Minor Mass and the two Passions, which he loved so much. Indeed, he wrote about the Mass in his 'Letter in May' of 1962. ...

Don't forget Hermann Hesse—everything is so quickly forgotten! It's a comfort to me to know how much you loved and still love him.

Your,
Ninon Hesse

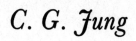

C. G. Jung

'We ought to find a new religious attitude.'

The Antarctic

In 1947 I took a trip to the Antarctic which I subsequently described in a book called *Invitation to the Ice Fields*. One thing I did not mention in that book, however, is that I took with me a book entitled *The Ego and the Unconscious* by Carl Gustav Jung. In a very real sense, that book interfered with the purpose of my journey, for the more I read in it, the less I observed the precise outlines of the icefields through which I was travelling. Only at the end of the voyage did I begin to realize, however dimly, that there was some relationship between that book and the distant lands which I had visited.

That was the first time that I had seriously encountered Jung's work. I had studied Freud and Adler but had only a superficial knowledge of Jung's book, *Psychological Types*. And then came this first real encounter. With his book in the pocket of my parka, I had slowly passed down along the length of Chile, enduring a constant rain as the ship passed by Patagonia, Tierra del Fuego, beyond the range of Ultima Esperanza, across the Beagle Strait and Drake's Sea to the great snow fields of the Antarctic. It was finally there, amongst gigantic icebergs reverberating with thunder as huge slabs of ice cracked off and fell into the sea, in an atmosphere of total whiteness burning with cold, that I turned my attention to Jung's book. There, in almost total isolation from the rest of the world, I began to look for something which would close that other gap which separates the Ego from the Subconscious in modern man.

It is hard for me now to look back on that time and place and to discover what it was in Jung's book that so interested me. But I imagine that it was the idea of the Archetype which there in the Antarctic seemed so real, and perhaps too the passing reference to Jesus and the suggestion that he had been caught in a world of brutal and autonomous forces not unlike the barren ice fields. The book revealed to me a whole frightening world, as terrifying as the white silence of the

Antarctic. It also seemed to strike a note in my own being,
calling forth ideas that I had dimly conceived, but which I
had not formulated.

When I returned from the Antarctic, it was difficult for me
to decide which had been more important for me, the trip or
Jung's book. Nevertheless, at that time, I didn't read anything
more by him. I was too caught up with the trip itself, going
over it again internally, in an attempt to understand its
connection with my own being. At that same time, I also
became increasingly anxious to travel to India in hopes of
discovering there the roots of South American legends and
myths. I was fascinated by the science of Yoga, which I had
already begun to study in Chile.

In the course of my thinking during those years, I had begun
to realise how difficult it was to translate the ancient wisdom
of myths and legends into a rational language. I therefore
turned again to Jung, and reread *The Ego and the Unconscious*.
From there, I went on to his commentaries on Chinese and
Tibetan Yoga. I read his commentary on *The Secret of the
Golden Flower*, his introduction to Richard Wilhelm's translation
of the *I Ching*, or *Book of Changes*; I also read his observations on
The Tibetan Book of the Great Liberation edited by Evans-Wentz
and his commentaries on *The Tibetan Book of the Dead*. I read
various of his alchemical works, such as his study of the
Rosarium Philosophorum, which is attributed to Petrus Toletanus,
and in addition studied his *Psychology and Religion, Aion*, and his
Symbols of Transformation. In much of this work, I noticed that
the Libido, which for Freud was synonomous with sex, for
Jung was something akin to the 'Kundalini' of Tantric Yoga.

The more I considered Jung's work, the more I became
conscious of a parallel, say, between his *Analytical Psychology*
and a path of initiation; it was as though there were a second
language underlying the first of which it is quite possible Jung
was not even aware. Thus the psychoanalyst came to be a
Guru, or Master, while the patient became a Chela or Disciple.
If sickness is in reality a divided or incomplete condition, and
health is totality, then Jung's treatment of the mentally ill
was an attempt to bring forth illusory phantoms and shadows
from the patient's past in order to create a new sense of reality
or of the Self, and this process closely parallels the teachings

of the Hindu Guru. Nevertheless, what Jung was really anxious to do was to establish a dialogue between the individual and the Universe, without destroying the idea of personality or the Ego.

During the years in which I lived in India, I learned about some extraordinary beings called Siddhas who had lived in the distant past. These people were alchemists and magicians and exercised enormous influence over India prior to the Aryan invasion. They had tried to maintain a dialogue between the Ego and the Self, but in place of the concept of *samadhi* propounded by the Vedantists, they attempted an even deeper state of trance, called *kaivalya*. This word means 'isolated' or 'separated,' and implies independence from the Universe, and even from God. The Siddhas tried to gain immortality within their own bodies, and used the alchemical combination of metals to do so.

My First Interview with Dr. Jung

IN DECEMBER OF 1957, I wrote to Dr. Jung, sending him an article I had written for *The Hindustan Times*. This article was entitled 'The Crucifixion of the Ego' and was inspired by a sentence I had heard in a speech by the then Vice-President of India, the philosopher Sarvapalli Radhakrishnan, who had spoken earlier that year to the world Congress of Religions in Delhi. Jung himself did not reply directly to my letter, but I learned through his secretary, Aniela Jaffe, that he had read the article. Because of overwork and ill health, he was not able to reply personally.

That period in India was for me a very strange one. I let the days pass by aimlessly, and I felt myself outside of time. My impressions of life about me were disjointed and passed by my consciousness like pieces of driftwood. From time to time I would sit in the lotus position and practice the Yoga of concentration. I concentrated particularly on the sacred syllable OM. To use Jung's terminology, I would say that those were years in which I was really fighting for my soul. At that time I wrote a story called *The Visits of the Queen of Sheba* but I

47

didn't know then that it was to be but the first of a number of
other stories like it, which were products of some strange disturbance within me. When I first met Jung, I gave him a copy
of that first work in which Oriental and Occidental symbols
were mixed and compounded with the 'legends' of my own life.

The importance of India in this relationship cannot be over-
emphasized. Without my Indian experience, it is probable
that I should never have been attracted to that great man, and
in the end, India was the link that joined us, since it had as
much importance for Jung as it had for Hesse. It was Mrs.
Indira Gandhi, Prime Minister Nehru's daughter, who had
first introduced me to Dorothy Norman, an intelligent American woman who was interested in Jung and in his work with
symbols. When Mrs. Norman learned that I wished to meet
Jung, she telegraphed Dr. Jolande Jacobi, one of Jung's
disciples in Zürich, asking her to try to arrange an interview.
Yet even with the help of Dr. Jacobi, it wasn't easy to meet
Jung in those days, since he was living in complete retirement.
When we met in Zürich, however, she told me that Dr. Jung
was vacationing in Locarno. Since I had to pass through
Locarno on my way to visit Hermann Hesse, I decided to try
to see him there.

And thus it was that I found myself on the afternoon of
February 28, 1959, standing in the large hall of the Hotel
Esplanade, in Locarno, waiting for Dr. Jung. I immediately
recognized him as he came down the central stairway. He was
tall but a little stoop-shouldered, had wispy white hair and
carried a pipe in his hand. He greeted me affably in English
and invited me to sit down with him in a corner by a balustrade
where we would be completely private.

'I understand you have just come from India,' he said. 'I was
there some time ago, trying to convince the Hindus that it
it impossible to get rid of the idea of the Ego or of consciousness, even in the deepest state of *samadhi*.'

Thus Dr. Jung immediately began on the central theme. His
gestures and words were solemn and elegant, but underneath
there was a burning enthusiasm which indicated his extraordinary vitality, even though at that time he was nearly
eighty-two years old.

Dr. Jung continued: 'When I was at the University of Calcutta in Bengal, I discussed this matter with various Brahman doctors and professors, but they were unable to understand. I tried to explain to them that if Ramakrishnan, for example, had been able to get rid of his consciousness completely in his moments of profound ecstasy, then those very moments would have been non-existent. He would never have been able to remember them or to record them, or even to consider them as having any existence at all.'

As he talked, I realized that I would have to keep myself very conscious of the moments that were passing between us, and I tried to be as observant as possible. I noticed that in addition to the energy which radiated from him while he talked, there was also in him a certain kindness, although it was some-times mixed with a sense of irony, or even of sarcasm. Yet above all, I was aware of a certain air of absence or mystery about him, for I knew that this kind man was quite capable of transforming himself into a cruel and destructive being if, by chance, certain of the extremes within him happened to fuse. His eyes were penetratingly observant; they seemed to see beyond his glasses, and perhaps beyond time. His nose was aquiline. I had seen a number of photographs of Jung showing him during his youth and mature years, but nothing connected those photographs with the person with whom I was sitting. I was struck with this transformation for Jung now looked like an ancient alchemist. His hands were knotty, like those of Hesse, and on the ring finger of his left hand, there was a dark stone mounted in gold and inscribed with strange characters.

Since our conversation had begun so pleasantly and cordially, it was destined to last much longer than I had thought it would. I also had the feeling that the interview was more like a meeting of old acquaintances than a first encounter. It was like meeting someone who was expecting you, and who you knew was expecting you. But to return to Dr. Jung's observations:

'Since the Unconscious really means the not-conscious, nobody can gain that state while he is alive, and be able to remember it afterwards, as the Hindus claim. In order to remember, one must have a conscious spectator, who is the Self or the conscious being. I discussed all this with the

Maharaja of Mysore's Guru. . . .' He paused and knocked his
pipe against the balustrade.

'I have always thought,' I said, 'that the Hindu tries to get
rid of the Ego in order to escape from the wheel of *Samsara*;
eternity for him would be like a continuous state of insomnia,
and he therefore wants to blend himself into the concept of
the Whole. That is what the modern Hindu wants, but as you
know the Siddhas tried something quite different. Now I
understand that you wish to establish a dialogue between the
Ego and that which transcends it, and that you wish to project
the light of consciousness more and more into the unconscious
. . . and that as a consequence you talk about the Collective
Unconscious; and I understand that by the law of
polarity, a Collective Conscious may also exist or even a Super-
conscious. Do you think that this is perhaps the state to which
the Hindu refers and to which he aspires when he undergoes
samhadi or, even more forcefully, *kaivalya*? Perhaps to gain that
state, to reach the Super-conscious, one has to get rid of every
day rational consciousness. Thus the difficulty between yourself and the Hindus may merely be one of misunderstanding,
or a failure to realize what the Hindu really means when he
says that he wishes to overcome the Ego.'

'That may well be,' said Jung, 'for the Hindus are notoriously
weak in rational exposition. They think for the most part in
parables or images. They are not interested in appealing to
reason. That, of course, is a basic condition of the Orient as a
whole. . . . As for your hypothesis about the Super-conscious,
that is a metaphysical concept and as a consequence outside
of my interests. I wish to proceed solely on facts and experiences. So far, I have found no stable or definite centre in the
unconscious and I don't believe such a centre exists. I believe
that the thing which I call the Self is an ideal centre, equidistant between the Ego and the Unconscious, and it is
probably equivalent to the maximum natural expression of
individuality, in a state of fulfilment or totality. As nature
aspires to express itself, so does man, and the Self is that dream
of totality. It is therefore an ideal centre, something created.
The Hindus have written wisely on this point. According to
the Sankya philosophers, the *Purusha* is the Self, and the *Atman*
may be similar to it. But the definition always takes the form

of a parable. Do you know the story of the disciple who went to visit his Master to ask him what the *Atman* was? The Master replied, "It is everything." But the disciple persisted: "Is it the Maharaja's elephant?" "Yes," answered the Master, "You are the *Atman* and so is the Maharaja's elephant." After that, the disciple departed very satisfied. On his way back, he met the Maharaja's elephant, but he did not move out of the road because he thought that if he and the elephant were both *Atman*, then the elephant would recognize him. Even when the elephant driver shouted at him to move, he refused to do so, and so the elephant picked him up with his trunk and threw him to the side. The next day, covered with bruises, the disciple once again called on his Master and said, "You told me that the elephant and I were both *Atman*, and now look what it has done to me." The Master remained perfectly calm and asked the disciple what the elephant driver had told him. "To get out of the way," answered the disciple. "You should have done what he told you to do," said the Master, "because the elephant driver is also *Atman*." Thus the Hindus have an answer for everything,' said Jung, laughing. 'They know a great deal. . . .'

'The Hindus live entirely in symbols,' I said, 'They are penetrated and inter-penetrated by them, but they don't interpret them, nor do they like anyone else to interpret them, since that would be like destroying them. I think that is why your work is not much known or discussed in India, even though you have devoted so much time to its culture and to the Orient in general. You interpret symbols. On the other hand, you are very well known and widely read in my own country.'

'I know, I am always receiving letters from Chile and from other countries in South America, and that surprises me since all of my work has been directed towards myself; all of the books that I have written are but by-products of an intimate process of *individuation*, even when they are connected by hermetic links to the past and, in all probability to the future. But since they are not supposed to be popular, and are not directed towards the masses, I am somewhat frightened by the sudden success I have had here and there. I am afraid it is not good, because real work is completed in silence and strikes a chord in the minds of only a very few. There is an old Chinese saying which states that if a man sitting alone in his own room thinks the right thoughts, he will be heard thousands of miles away. . . .'

Dr. Jung remained quiet for a moment before continuing:

'Yes, India is an extraordinarily interesting country, and you should live that experience *right*, and you should live it intensely until the hour comes. . . . I also wanted to confront that universe and, as a product of the Christian West, to use it to test my own ways, and to give life to those zones within me which correspond to those of the Hindus, but which in the West for the most part remain dormant. And that is why I went to India in 1938. Let me tell you what I now think of that country, and you can correct me later. So far as I can see, an Indian, so long as he remains an Indian, doesn't *think*—at least in the same way we do. Rather, he *perceives* a thought. In this way, the Indian approximates primitive ways of thinking. I don't say that the Indian is primitive, but merely that the processes of his thought remind me of primitive methods of producing thoughts. Primitive reasoning is in essence an unconscious function which only perceives immediate results. We can only hope to find that kind of reasoning in a civilization which has progressed virtually without interruption from primitive times. Our natural evolution in Western Europe was broken by the introduction of a psychology and of spirituality which had developed from a civilization higher than our own. We were interrupted at the very beginning when our beliefs were still barbarously polytheistic, and these beliefs were forced underground and have remained there for the last two thousand years. That I believe explains the divisiveness that is found in the Western mind. Still in a primitive state, we were forced to adopt the comparatively sophisticated doctrines of Christian grace and love. A dissociation was thus produced in Western man between the conscious and the unconscious part of his mentality. The conscious mind was undoubtedly freed from irrationality and instinctive impulses, but total individuality was lost. Western man became someone divided between his conscious and unconscious personality. The conscious personality could always be domesticated because it was separated from the primitive, and as a consequence we in the West have come to be highly disciplined, organized and rational. On the other hand, having allowed our unconscious personality to be suppressed, we are excluded from an understanding or appreciation of the primitive man's education and civilization. Nevertheless, our unconscious personality still exists and occasionally erupts in an uncontrolled fashion. Thus we are capable of relapsing into the most shocking barbarisms and, the more successful we become in science and technology, the more diabolical are the uses to which we put our inventions and discoveries.

'But to make man aware of his conscious side is not the only way to civilize him, and in any case, is not the ideal way. A far more satisfactory approach would be to consider man as a whole instead of considering his various parts. What is needed is to call a halt to the fatal dissociation that exists between man's higher and lower being; instead, we must unite conscious man with primitive man. In India we can find a civilization which has incorporated everything that is essential to primitivism and, as a consequence, we find man considered as a whole. The civilization and psychology of India are well-represented in their temples, because these temples represent the Universe. I make this point in particular in order to explain what I mean by *not thinking*. What I mean is simply that, thank God, there is still a man who has not learned how to think, but who still perceives his thoughts as though they were visions or living beings, and who perceives his gods as though they were visible thoughts, based on instinctive reality. He has made peace with his gods, and they live with him. It is true that the life he leads is close to nature. It is full of hope, of brutality, misery, sickness and death; nevertheless, it has a completeness, a satisfaction and an emotional beauty which is unfathomable. Undoubtedly, the logic of this civilization is imperfect, and thus we see fragments of Western science side by side with what we call superstition. But if these contradictions are improbable to us, they are not to the Indians. If these contradictions exist, they are merely the peculiarities of autonomous thought and are responsible only to themselves. The Indian himself is not responsible for these contradictions, since his thought *comes to him*. This phenomenon is illustrated by the Indian's lack of interest in the details of the Universe. He is only interested in having a vision of totality. But alas, he does not realize that the living world can be destroyed in a struggle between two concepts. . . .'

Professor Jung paused, leaned back against the chair and seemed to be looking at some distant point—perhaps at his image of the Indian.

'Yes,' I said, 'that is what India is like. It is a great natural civilization, or rather, a civilization of nature. Indeed, it could be said of all of the Orient that, at least until very recently, it has not tried to *dominate* nature, but to respect its laws and to understand them—to give them a meaning. Nevertheless, it has no sense of *persona*; it only knows the archetype. I realize, of course, that the idea of personality is not necessarily good; perhaps it's quite the opposite. . . .'

'Yes, India is archetypal,' said Jung. 'And that is why I made no plans to visit Swamis or Gurus when I went to India; I didn't even go to see Ramana Maharishi, who had so interested Somerset Maugham, because I felt that it was not necessary to do so. I knew what a Swami was; I had an exact idea of his archetype; and that was enough to know them all, especially in a world where extreme personal differentiation doesn't exist as it does in the West. We have more variety, but it's only superficial. . . .'

After a moment of silence, I then spoke:

'You said, Dr. Jung, that you went to India in order to know yourself better. I went to do something like that myself, because I want to discover what we South Americans are. We are neither Asian nor are we European. You have said that the Hindu doesn't *think* his thoughts, and I take that to mean that he doesn't think with his mind, with his brain, but that his thoughts are produced in some other centre of his being. Do you think that is possible? It has always seemed to me that we South Americans do not *think* from the rational centre, but from some other one, and consequently, our first task is to discover what that other centre is, so that we can begin to understand our own being. Where do you suppose this centre is located? Do you think we should take seriously the hypothesis of the *chakras*—the pyschic centres of Yoga?'

'Your question is very interesting,' answered Jung. 'I once remember having a conversation with the chief of the Pueblo Indians, whose name was Ochwiay Biano, which means

7. C. G. Jung in his study, wearing his gnostic ring.

the Americans also. Therefore they should not interfere with our religion. But if they continue to do so (by missionaries) and hinder us, then they will see, that in ten years the Sun will rise no more."

He correctly assumes, that their day, their light, their consciousness and their meaning will die, when destroyed through the narrowmindedness of American Rationalism, and the same will happen to the whole world, when subjected to such treatment. That is the reason, why I tried to hold the best truth with the clearest light I could attain to and since I have reached my highest point I can't transcend anymore, I am guarding my light and my treasure, convinced that nobody would gain and I myself would be badly even hopelessly injured, if I should loose it. It is most precious not only to me, but above all to the darkness of the Creator, who needs man to illuminate his creation. If God had foreseen his world, it would be a mere, senseless machine and Man's existence a useless freak.

My intellect can envisage the latter possibility, but the whole of my being says "no" to it.

Sincerely yours

C.G. Jung

8. Final page of Jung's long letter to the author.

Mountain Lake. He gave me his impressions of the white man, and he said that they were always upset, always looking for something, and that as a consequence, their faces were lined with wrinkles, which he took to be a sign of eternal restlessness. Ochwiay Biano also thought that the whites were crazy since they maintained that they thought with their heads, whereas it was well-known that only crazy people did that. This assertion by the chief of the Pueblos so surprised me that I asked him how *he* thought. He answered that he naturally thought with his heart.'

And then Jung added: 'And that is how the ancient Greeks also thought.'

'That is extraordinary,' I said. 'The Japanese, you know, consider the centre of the person to be in the solar plexus. But do you believe that white people think with their heads?'

'No. They think only with their tongues.' Jung then placed his hand on his neck. 'They think only with words, with words which today have replaced the Logos. . . .'

'But what about the *chakras*, Doctor, what do you think about them? Some people claim that they correspond to the plexes of Western science. At the very least, they seem to be located in the same places as the plexes are. Of course the Tantric yogis say that the *chakras* and the nadis are psychic centres, rather than physiological or physical, and that they are located along a "vertebral column" which is also psychic. Thus the *chakras* only exist potentially; they come into being only by an act of the will, usually through the practice of Yoga. Perhaps they are something like the Self, which you mentioned a few moments ago—something which must be created. In any event, many questions remain to be answered about that ancient Oriental science, and many of the techniques now seem to be lost, perhaps in some huge cataclysm which overtook their civilization.'

'The *chakras*,' said Jung, 'are centres of consciousness, and Kundalini, the Fiery Serpent, which is to be found at the base of the spine, is an emotional current that runs along the spine, uniting what is below with what is above, and vice versa.'

Dr. Jung then paused in an effort to remember the Sanskrit

names of the various *chakras*. 'I am very old now, and am losing my memory,' he said. My own impression, on the contrary, was that his memory was prodigious.

'Starting from the bottom,' he said, 'at the base of the vertebral column is the *Muladhara chakra*; then in the solar plexus comes the *Manipura*; after that there is the *Anahata*, which is in the heart, the *Vishuda*, which is in the throat, the *Ajna* which is found at a point between the eyebrows, and finally there is the *Brahma-chakra*, which is the coronary *chakra*. These locations are useful only to give you an idea of what I mean. The *chakras* are centres of consciousness. The lower ones represent animal consciousness, and there are even others below the Muladhara.'

'I suppose that if we were able to activate all of these centres, we would then achieve totality,' I said. 'Still, that would probably bring about the end of history which seems to be like a pendular movement from one *chakra* to another. That is to say, each civilization seems to express a particular *chakra*, and different types of consciousness exist in various parts of the world and at various times.' I then asked Dr. Jung whether he could define his concept of the Self and what he believed to be the real centre of personality.

'The Self,' said Jung, 'is a circle whose centre is everywhere and whose circumference is nowhere.' Dr. Jung spoke that sentence in Latin. 'And do you know what the Self is for Western man? It is Christ, for Christ is the archetype of the hero, representing man's highest aspiration. All this is very mysterious and at times frightening.' Jung then fell silent for a moment.

I then gave Dr. Jung a copy of an English translation of my story, *The Visits of the Queen of Sheba*, which I had brought especially for him. I had written a special dedication to him in Spanish.

Just then three people came up to us, one of them a woman dressed in black. She reminded Jung that it was time for dinner, and I then realized how quickly the time had passed. I rose to leave and shook him by the hand, without knowing whether we would ever meet again and with a realization that we had so many more things to talk about. He said good-bye and I walked out into the dazzling lights of the city of Locarno.

May 5, 1959: Second Interview

ON THE FOLLOWING DAY I went to Montagnola to see Hermann Hesse, and upon my return I decided that I should try to see Dr. Jung again. I rang him up at his house in Küsnacht which is near Zürich, because I knew that by that time he had returned from his holidays. There was a certain risk in that telephone call, because I knew that Dr. Jung was receiving no visitors; but if I had not made it, my relationship with Jung would undoubtedly have ceased. His secretary, Aniela Jaffe, with whom I had corresponded from India, answered the phone. She was very doubtful about my request and insisted that Professor Jung was receiving no one and that he was not in good health. I then told her that I had been with him in Locarno and pleaded with her to ask whether I might come. Mrs. Jaffe put down the phone, and a few moments later returned to tell me that Jung would receive me at four o'clock that very afternoon.

I left immediately and arrived in time at his house in Küsnacht. Over the doorway of his house was written an inscription in Latin: 'Vocatus adque non vocatus, Deus aderit.' (Called or not called, God is present.)

The inside of the house seemed dark and shadowy. I was greeted by the same woman I had seen with Jung in Locarno and she introduced herself as Miss Bailey. She asked me to go up, and as I climbed the stairs, I noticed that the walls were covered with ancient drawings of medieval and Renaissance scenes. I then waited in a little room upstairs.

In due course Dr. Jung appeared and greeted me cordially, asking me to go into his study which had a window overlooking the lake. In the centre of the room was a desk covered with papers, and round about were many bookcases. I noticed some bronze Buddhas and over his work table a large scroll showing Siva on top of Mount Kailas. That painting forcibly reminded me of the many pilgrimages which I myself had taken into the Himalayas. We sat down beside the window, and Dr. Jung made himself comfortable in a large armchair opposite me.

'Your story about the Queen of Sheba is more like a poem

57

than an ordinary tale,' he said. 'The affair of the King and
the Queen of Sheba seems to contain everything; it has a
truly noumenal quality.'

I listened quietly and he continued:

'But if you should ever meet the Queen of Sheba in the
flesh, beware of marrying her. The Queen of Sheba is only for
a magic kind of love, never for matrimony. If you were to
marry her, you would both be destroyed and your soul would
disintegrate.'

'I know,' I answered.

'In my long psychiatric experience I never came across a
marriage that was entirely self-sufficient. Once I thought I
had, because a German professor assured me that his was. I
believed him until once, when I was visiting in Berlin, I discovered that his wife kept a secret apartment. That seems to
be the rule. Moreover, a marriage which is devoted entirely
to mutual understanding is bad for the development of individual personality; it is a descent to the lowest common
denominator, which is something like the collective stupidity
of the masses. Inevitably, one or the other will begin to penetrate the mysteries. Look, it's like this. . . .'

Jung then picked up a box of matches and opened it. He
separated the two halves and placed them on a table so that
at a distance they looked the same. He then brought them together until the drawer of the box entered the shell.

'That's how it is,' he said; 'the two halves appear equal, but
in fact they are not. Nor should they be, since one should
always be able to include the other or, if you like, remain
outside of the other. Ideally, the man should contain the
woman and remain outside of her. But it's a question of degree,
and the homosexual is fifty-five per cent feminine. Basically
speaking, however, man is polygamous. The people of the
Mussulman Empire knew that very well. Nevertheless, marrying several women at the same time is a primitive solution,
and would be rather expensive today.'

Jung then laughed before continuing:

'I think that the French have found the solution in the
Number Three. Frequently this number occurs in magic
marriages such as your encounter with the Queen of Sheba.
It is something quite different from Freud's sexual interpre-

tations or from D. H. Lawrence's ideas. Freud was wrong, for example, in his interpretation of incest which, in Egypt, was primarily religious and had to do with the process of individuation. In reality, the King was the individual, and the people were merely an amorphous mass. Thus the King had to marry his mother or his sister in order to protect and preserve individuality in the country. Lawrence exaggerated the importance of sex because he was excessively influenced by his mother; he over-emphasized women because he was still a child and was unable to integrate himself in the world. People like him frequently suffer from respiratory illnesses which are primarily adolescent. Another curious case is that of Saint-Exupéry: from his wife I learned many important details about him. Flight, you see, is really an act of evasion, an attempt to escape from the earth. But the earth must be accepted and admitted, perhaps even sublimated. That is frequently illustrated in myth and religion. The dogma of the Ascension of Mary is in fact an acceptance of matter; indeed it is a sanctification of matter. If you were to analyse dreams, you would understand this better. But you can see it also in alchemy. It's a pity we have no alchemical texts written by women, for then we would know something essential about the visions of women, which are undoubtedly different from those of men.'

I then asked Dr. Jung whether he thought it was wise to analyse one's own dreams and to pay attention to them. I told him that I had begun to analyse my own again and that I'd found my vitality increasing, as though I were making use of some hidden sources of energy which otherwise would have been lost. 'On the other hand,' I said, 'I have talked with Krishna Murti, in India, and he told me that dreams have no real importance, and that the only important thing is *to look*, to be conscious and totally aware of the moment. He told me that he never dreams. He said that because he looks with both his conscious and unconscious mind, he has nothing left over for dreams, and that when he sleeps he gains complete rest.'

'Yes, that is possible for a time,' said Jung. 'Some scientists have told me that when they were concentrating with all their attention on a particular problem, they no longer dreamed. And then, for some unexplained reason, they began to dream again. But to return to your question about the importance of analysing your own dreams, it seems to me that the only important thing is to follow nature. A tiger should be a good tiger; a tree, a good tree. So man should be man. But to know what man is, one must follow nature and go on alone, admitting the importance of the unexpected. Still, nothing is possible without love, not even the processes of alchemy, for love puts one in a mood to risk everything and not to withhold important elements.'

Jung then rose and took a volume from the bookcase. It was his own *Archetypes of the Collective Unconscious*, and he opened it to a chapter called 'Study of a Process of Individuation'. He showed me the extraordinary coloured plates that are reproduced there, some of Tibetan tankas.

'These were made,' he said, 'by a woman with whom we planned a process of individuation for almost ten years. She was an American and had a Scandinavian mother.' He pointed to one picture done in bright colours. In the centre was a flower, rather like a four-leaf clover, and above it were drawn a king and queen who were taking part in a mystic wedding, holding fire in their hands. There were towers in the background.

'The process of the mystic wedding involves various stages,' Jung explained, 'and is open to innumerable risks, like the *Opus Alquimia*. For this union is in reality a process of mutual individuation which occurs, in cases like this, in both the doctor and the patient.'

As he spoke of this magic love and alchemic wedding, I thought of Solomon and the Queen of Sheba, Christ and his Church, and of Siva and Parvati on the summit of Mount Kailas—all symbols of man and his soul and of the creation of the Androgynous.

Jung went on as though he were talking to himself: 'Somewhere there was once a Flower, a Stone, a Crystal, a Queen, a King, a Palace, a Lover and his Beloved, and this was long ago, on an Island somewhere in the ocean five thousand years ago. . . . Such is Love, the Mystic Flower of the Soul. This is the Centre, the Self. . . .'

Jung spoke as though he were in a trance.

'Nobody understands what I mean;' he said, 'only a poet could begin to understand. . . .'

'You are a poet,' I said, moved by what I had heard. 'And that woman, is she still alive?' I asked.

'She died eight years ago. . . . I am very old. . . .'

I then realized that the interview should end. I had brought Hermann Hesse's book, *Piktor's Metamorphosis*. I showed him the drawings and gave him greetings from Steppenwolf.

'I met Hesse through a mutual friend who was interested in myths and symbols,' said Jung. 'His friend worked with me for a while, but he was unable to follow through to the end. The path is very difficult. . . .'

It was late when I left Jung's house, and as I walked down towards the lake, I thought of our conversation and tried to put my feelings in order.

Magic Weddings

As I WALKED ALONG, I wondered whether there was a second language in the process of individuation discovered by Jung. I knew that if I were to ask him, he would deny it. But even so, I am sure that such a language exists. It seems to be there, waiting to be discovered. There is a difference between what a man does and what happens, by itself. I have discovered this in many parts of the world, in buildings, in works of art, and in the lives of certain people who have achieved greatness in spite of themselves. A man will set himself to a task with determination and tenacity, and then suddenly a gust of wind will come from another world, and everything changes. He seems to be used by the gods; in spite of himself, he is a part of the Myth. Jung's work has been too tenacious and dramatic for his line not to be carried on into the future. As one who revitalized the work of the Gnostics and the alchemists, he himself had to take part in their mysteries, even though he may originally have intended to remain outside of them. For neither the Gnostics nor the alchemists created symbols for the sake of psychological analysis, but for the sake of magic itself. And that means that even though he fought against it, Jung condemned himself to be a magician who was willing to pass beyond the frontiers of official science in our time. I think he realized that when he said that only poets could understand him.

In philosophic alchemy, there exists the idea of the *Soror Mystica* who works with the alchemist while he mixes his substances in his retorts. She is with him at all times throughout the long process of fusion, and at the end, there occurs a mystic wedding, involving the creation of the Androgynous. This could not have occurred without the presence of the woman, without, in short, the psychic encounter of the Sister and the Alchemist.

In the processes of individuation worked out in the Jungian laboratory between the patient and the analyst, the same fusion takes place. Images and dreams are produced between the two, and become common to both of them so that neither remembers who it was that first produced the dream or the image. This psychic union never takes place in ordinary love, for even though two lovers may wish to fuse themselves completely, they will never be able to dream the same dream; there will always be something that separates them. The magic wedding is alone capable of closing the gap. Jung said that this psychic union could only take place in a spirit of love, since only then would one be willing to risk everything. Nevertheless, the love of the psychic union is tricky and dangerous; it is a love without love, contrary to the laws of physical creation and history. It is a forbidden love, which can only be fulfilled outside of matrimony. This love for the Queen of Sheba, then, does not produce a child of flesh, but a child of spirit, or of the imagination. It is a fusion of opposing factors within the psyche of each of the lovers; it is a process of magical individuation. While it is true that this love does not exclude physical love, the physical becomes transformed into ritual. What *is* excluded is mutual sexual pleasure.

The best way of explaining this complicated idea is to consider the Tantric practices of India, in which the Siddha magicians attempted to achieve psychic union. The ritual of the Tantras is complicated and mysterious. The initiate had to be chaste, and the woman would usually be one of the sacred prostitutes of the temples which in reality is the same as being chaste. A long period of preparation was required before the culmination of the ritual. The man and the woman would go off together into the forest, living like brother and sister, like the alchemist and his sister, exchanging ideas, images and words. They would sleep together in the same bed, but they would not touch each other. Only after months of preparation would the final Tantric Mass take place, in which wine was drunk, meat and cereal eaten, and finally *Maithuna*, or mystical coitus performed. This act was the culmination of the long process of sublimation, during which the flesh was transformed and transfigured, just as in alchemy lead is converted into gold, and the act of coitus was really intended to ignite the mystic fire at the base of the vertebral column.

This inextinguishable fire is the product of supreme love, but it has nothing whatever to do with the ordinary sexual act, in which something physical dies in order to produce a new life of flesh. In this love, the spirit of death is operative and produces a life of spirit. The woman is a priestess of magic love, whose function is to touch and awaken the various *chakras* of the Tantric hero, who is thus permitted to reach new levels of consciousness until totality is achieved. In the end, the pleasure that is gained is not one of the ejaculation of semen, which is strictly prohibited, but is the pleasure of vision, of the opening of the Third Eye, which represents the fusion of opposites. The man does not ejaculate the semen, but impregnates himself; and thus the process of creation is reversed and time is stopped. The product of this forbidden love is the Androgynous, the Total Man, all of whose *chakras*, or centres of consciousness, are now awakened. It is an encounter with the Self, that Last Flower of the soul on an Island five thousand years ago. . . .

Once this rite of love without love is completed, the man and the woman separate. They are now complete and individuated. In this Tantric Mass the man has in fact married his spirit; he has married with Anima and she, with Animus.

On the walls of the temple of Khajuraho, in India, this forbidden love is pictured in thousands of sculptured figures. But nowhere are there statues of children, and that is why this love is an unnatural love. Inside the temple, in a most secret place, sits Siva the Androgynous, meditating with his eyes closed, considering and enjoying his own act of creation.

In India, the meaning of this forbidden love is reiterated in the story of Krishna, the blue god, so loved by Hesse, who danced with his loves in the gardens of Vrindavan. His chief lover was Radha, who was a married woman, and with her was realized the Number Three while they danced within a *mandala* and attained the Self.

In these strange rites, it is not important that the *Maithuna* be physical; what is important is that the Mystic Sister be there, with the alchemist, helping him to mix his substances and, like Mary Magdalen, aiding him in his hour of greatest need. What counts, then, is the psychic interplay of the two, of the patient with the analyst, to create together and to find themselves in this process of individuation.

The final wedding, or union, takes place within the isolated individual, who is so completely alone that he really has no sense at all of his own body. This union is achieved by Kundalini, which Jung defined as an 'emotional current'. Like the mercury of the alchemists or the 'astral fire' of the occultists, Kundalini awakens the *chakras* one by one until finally the Third Eye, or *Ajna Chakra* is opened and the *Brahma Chakra* or Final Emptiness is achieved. It is a wedding between the Ego and the Self achieved through a union of the Anima with the Animus. From the hand of Beatrice, Dante descended to the Inferno and then ascended to Heaven. . . .

'Only poets will be able to understand me. . . .' I realized now the force of Jung's words; I realized too that Jung, the magician, had almost alone made it possible for us today to take part in those Mysteries which seem capable of taking us back to that legendary land of the Man-God.

And now we must wait for the appearance of a disciple capable of propounding his message, interpreting the underlying language of his work, which is already there like a palimpsest. That disciple will have to be a priest, a magician or a poet.

With Dr. Jacobi

BEFORE LEAVING ZÜRICH, I wanted to thank Dr. Jolande Jacobi for the help she had given me. I therefore went to visit her at her apartment. She was most interested to hear of my talks with Dr. Jung and questioned me closely. She was particularly anxious to know whether he had spoken of the world situation.

'Jung is very much afraid that a war or catastrophe will take place in 1964,' she said, 'because in that year, the world moves from one epoch into another. The coming of Christ coincided with the beginning of the present era, Pisces, which is now nearing its end.'

I told her that he had said nothing about this.

'Jung is also fascinated by the coming of beings from other worlds in outer space, and he equates them with the collective visions of flying saucers which have been experienced in so many parts of the world. He believes that humanity is about to undergo an enormous change.'

'Jung didn't mention any of this,' I said. 'We talked about *chakras*. He said that they were centres of consciousness, and that Kundalini is the emotional current which unites them.'

'No,' she said, '*chakras* are centres of energy and the Kundalini of Yoga represents the development of psychical energy. . . .'

'We also talked of the interpretation of dreams,' I said, 'and I told him that my vitality seemed to increase when I analysed my own dreams.'

'That's logical,' she replied, 'because you are really conserving energy which otherwise would be lost. But it is extremely difficult to analyse your own dreams accurately.'

I then asked Dr. Jacobi what she thought of Archetypes.

'The Archetype is something like the structure of the psyche or an impulse that has a certain universal form, but in fact no one knows where the idea originated.'

'Do you think that there is a counterpart to the Collective Unconscious?' I asked.

'On the social level, Europe and America are Collective Consciousnesses with their legislature and laws. International law is a form of Collective Consciousness which balances and which is polarized by the primitiveness of the people of Asia and Africa. On the one hand, you have the rational, and on the other, the barbarous. And the rational seeks to regulate the earth and to escape from it; that is, the rational is frustrated in its attempt to regulate the world, and as a consequence wishes to escape from it. Thus the airplane is a symbol of the West, and the more pilots there are, the fewer men. And thanks to automation, the pilot has already become a kind of feminine man. . . .'

65

Over a glass of vermouth, we then spoke about India. Professor Jacobi thought of it simply as a place where the *Persona* is annihilated in order that it might be merged with the *Atman,* and she was opposed to this Vedantic idea. Instead, she supported Jungian psychology with its desire to establish a dialogue between man and his personal god, or between the Ego and the Self. 'That does not mean that God exists,' she said. 'Jung wishes to widen the radius of consciousness, extending it into regions which are still shadowy, and thus completing the work of creation, and *finishing what Nature left incomplete.* . . . No one in the West tries to be a god as in India; rather, the mystic Christian connects himself with God on one day, and then on the following day he eats his breakfast. His life is something simple; it is merely a product of faith.'

It was clear from what she said that Dr. Jacobi did not like India. She was then sixty-nine years old, and we talked about Wilhelm and about Count Keyserling. She had known Keyserling and considered him to be an exceptional person. 'When he was here,' she said, 'it was impossible to talk with him, because he himself was a volcano of words. He has been here many times, sitting in the very chair you are sitting in.'

When it was time to leave Zürich, I wrote to Jung, thanking him, and this is what I said:

My conversations with you were of profound significance for me. Those days seemed to be full of meaning and to have had an almost magical quality. I shall never forget our talk about love in your house at Küsnacht.

All the time during our conversations I felt the presence of the Queen of Sheba hovering round us. She and I had met only recently, but I had the feeling that you had known her for a long time. And I take the liberty of saying that since both of us have met this Queen in our own lives, eternity will drink a toast to us on the far side of life and death.

Thus I send all my thanks to you in memory of our Queens of Sheba, who are perhaps one and the same.

Dr. Jung Writes a Preface
for My Book

I FELT INSPIRED by my encounter with Dr. Jung, and when I returned to India, I worked hard on my stories about the Queen of Sheba. They began to take shape almost of their own accord, and I felt that they were almost writing themselves. I sensed that I was merely being used so that these stories might be written.

During all that time, I felt as though I were caught in a net or, to use another image, that I was afloat on the sea of the Collective Unconscious. I had the impression that I was being beaten by powerful winds, stronger even than those of the monsoon, and in the warm summer nights, heavy with the perfume of jasmine, I felt as though I were reaching back to remote times, and that the old flute which I could hear outside my window really came from Ur in Chaldea, or from the legendary Iskandaria in the plains of Central Asia. I tried to recreate these myths in terms of flesh and blood, but in the end what came was a bloody foot, a wound in the side, a cross, and a Flower over the Cross.

Once the book was finished and translated into English, I sent it to Professor Jung in Küsnacht, accompanied by the following letter:

Delhi,
November 26, 1959

Dear Dr. Jung,

I am certain that you are the only person who can properly understand these pages which I am sending to you. They were written originally in Spanish and are now translated into English. In a sense they were inspired by yourself since they begin with the 'The Visit of the Queen of Sheba' which I gave you in Locarno last February. Your understanding encouraged me to complete the work with these new stories, and I have had them translated into English so that you can read them. I am sending you the book in manuscript form before having it published here in India. I will be most grate-

67

ful for any suggestions that you may have, and my only hope is that you will have time to read it.

Nearly two months passed before I received the following letter:

> *Küsnacht-Zürich,*
> *Seestrasse 228*
> *January 14, 1960*

Dear Mr. Serrano,

Will you please excuse my long silence! Old age slows down the *tempo* of all activities and finally I had to wait for a spell of time, when I could retire from the vicinity of the town to the quietness and silence of the country where I can write a letter without disturbance.

Your MS is an extraordinary piece of work. It is dreams within dreams, highly poetic I should say and most unlike the spontaneous products of the unconscious I am used to, although well-known archetypic figures are clearly discernible. The poetic genius has transformed the primordial material into almost musical shapes, as, on the other side, Schopenhauer understands Music as the movement of archetypic ideas. The chief moulding and shaping factor seems to be a strong aesthetical tendency. Consequently the effect on the reader captivates him in an increasing dream, in an ever-extending space and an immeasurable depth of time. On the other hand, the cognitive element plays no significant rôle; it even recedes into a misty background yet alive with a wealth of colourful images. The unconscious or whatever we designate by this name presents itself to you by its poetic aspect, which I envisage chiefly from its scientific and philosophic—or perhaps more accurate—from its religious aspect. The Unconscious is surely the *Pammeter*, the Mother of All (i.e., of all psychical life), being the matrix, the background and foundation of all the differentiated phenomena we call psychical: religion, science, philosophy and art. Its experience—in whatever form it may be —is an approach to wholeness, the one experience absent in our modern civilization. It is the avenue and via regia to the Unus Mundus.

My best wishes for the New Year!

> Sincerely yours,
> C. G. JUNG

What struck me in particular from that letter were the sentences in which Jung defined himself, saying that the Unconscious presented itself most forcefully to him in its religious aspect.

I showed Dr. Jung's letter to several friends, most of whom were in favour of my asking Dr. Jung if I could use it as a Preface. I resisted this impulse, partly because I did not want to bother him, and partly because I believe that small plants never grow in the shade of great trees. I also felt that it was wrong to use this letter as a prop, because I believed that I should go on alone as he himself had done.

At that period, the English historian Arnold Toynbee was in New Delhi, and one day I asked him to lunch. We were talking of Jung, and Toynbee told me that it was while he was reading Jung that he himself decided to search for a mythical explanation for the civilizations of the world. I showed him Jung's letter and asked whether he thought I should ask for its use as a Preface. Toynbee was dubious, but it was in fact that very conversation with him in which he confessed that the reading of Jung had inspired him in his own work, that made me decide to write Jung and ask him whether I might use his letter as a Preface.

Dr. Jung's reply came quickly, almost as though he had been waiting for my request, and I had the feeling that he had in fact written the first letter in hopes that it would be used as a Preface.

Küsnacht-Zürich
Seestrasse 228
June 16, 1960

Dear Mr. Serrano,

Thank you for your kind letter. I feel the pangs of bad conscience very vividly indeed since I have not yet found the necessary time and leisure to answer your previous letter which I had the honour to receive quite a while ago. In cases like that, I always have to wait for the *kairos*, the right moment of time, when I am able to give a profound reply. But lately I have been disturbed by so many things and, above all, importunate visitors, that the favourable occasion to answer has not presented itself. But I am carrying your letter with the firm intention to write as soon as it is possible, and you shall get an answer in time.[1]

[1] The letter and the reply referred to are reproduced further on in this work.

Now as to your request, I am happy to say that I should appreciate very much seeing my letter included in your book.

May I call your attention to an error in printing? The Greek name of the Mother of All is correctly written *Pammeter* and not *Panmeter*.

I hear to my great regret that you suffered from an accident, a parallel, as one might say, to the terrible disaster that has befallen your country. We are reading with horror about the enormous destructions and the great loss of lives. It seems that Mother Earth is involved in a similar predicament as mankind, although the scientific mind does not sympathize with such coincidences.[1]

I have not begun yet my summer vacation. I am still trying to fight my way out of the submerging flood of work.

My best wishes to your speedy recovery!

Yours sincerely,
C. G. JUNG

This then, is the story of Dr. Jung's collaboration with me in a symbolic and poetical work. I don't believe that in all his long life he wrote another Preface for a purely literary work. Such introductions as he did write were for scientific works or translations like the *I Ching* and *The Golden Flower* by Wilhelm, or for the *Tibetan Book of the Dead* and *The Tibetan Book of the Great Liberation*. Why was it that Jung wrote this Preface for me? Was it an example of synchronicity—or was it in response to

[1] Reference to the 1960 earthquakes in Chile. At that time I answered Jung in this way: 'I am sure that there must exist a profound relationship between Mother Earth and man's mind. At times I think that the earth is a great body, and that man is something like the cells of that body. When you wrote to me about my accident, you made me think that it was *parallel* to the terrible disaster which is still taking place in my country.

'The fantastic beauty of the Chilean countryside, its mountains and lakes and the extraordinary transparency of the air round the snow-covered volcanoes, reminds one of the beauty of a soul living on the edge of an abyss, or of that strange light which emanates from a girl ill with tuberculosis, who must inevitably die.

'Yes, Chile is an extraordinary point on the body of Mother Earth, and my whole being is involved in that country. In reality, I am a man from the south of the World.'

(Extract from a letter written to Jung, June 27, 1960.)

70

an impulse from the Hermetic Circle, the Aurea Catena, which has no age? . . .

When the first copy of my book came off the press I sent it to Jung with the following inscription:

> If sometimes I wonder whether occult forces actually inter-
> vene in the world, the fact that you have written this prologue
> for *The Visits* proves their existence. It is also a *visit* from the
> mysterious unknown in which we are bound together. Perhaps
> we have always been together through the will of someone
> whom we don't know but who knows us.

New Delhi
Sunday, August 21, 1960.

With Arnold Toynbee

As I HAVE ALREADY SAID, Arnold Toynbee was visiting India at that time. He had been invited by the Indian Council for Cultural Relations and gave several talks at a seminary named in honour of Maulana Azad. In these lectures, Toynbee spoke of the necessity for universal religion, and about the need for establishing a *modus vivendi* which would allow all of the world's religious groups to exist peacefully side by side.

What has always interested Toynbee is the fact that although man has existed on earth for more than a million years, civilization began only five thousand years ago. He is con-cerned to know why it did not come earlier and wonders what preceded it. The Jungian hypothesis of archetypes, and of the universal myth, gave Toynbee a beginning. As he said to me, 'Perhaps some tribal chieftain had a dream which over-powered him. He became possessed by the Myth, by an arche-type, and through fear or wonder transmitted it to the whole community.'

Thus for Toynbee, religion is the prime motivation in history. And in fact, religion is always revealed in terms of images which have universal meaning, and which reappear in the course of history. He believes that science and technology have finally made possible the emergence of a universal religion; and that is why he approves of scientific development. My own view is that science overemphasizes the rational and thus produces the reverse effect.

I asked Toynbee what he conceived the Archetype to be. He answered that it was quite different from the Platonic Idea, and that it was a natural phenomenon. Toynbee confessed, however, that he was never able to understand Jung's hypothesis of synchronism. We then talked about the beginning of history in Europe and Asia, and Toynbee told me that he had visited several countries in South America because of his interest in pre-Columbian civilization.

I told him that I thought the West was now interested in rediscovering the values of the soul, while the East was beginning to experience technology and the results of a purely extroverted civilization. I said that I thought this development posed a tremendous threat for the white man who would have to face the expansion of the many coloured races all over the world. The only solution for the white man was to dive under, like a swimmer when confronted by a huge wave, in order to come out on the other side. I felt that he ought to keep quiet and allow the coloured races to speak. The white man would also have to withdraw somewhat, in order to preserve a legacy for the future. This, I felt, was the only possible way to deal with the millions of hitherto oppressed people who have a just desire for vengeance. This act of diving under should not be merely a political or social act, but a spiritual one in which the white man tries to rediscover his Myth and Legend. Only in this way would the white man preserve the essence of his civilization. What was needed most of all, then, was work of individual perfection. And success in this line depended upon the realization of magic. In social terms it involved the emergence in the West of strong individualists capable of equalizing the incoherent movements of the masses.

I then said that the East, by contrast, had a completely different problem because it had exhausted the methods of introversion. Yoga, meditation and concentration were no longer able to produce results because the Collective Unconscious of the East was no longer in tune with it. Instead, the Eastern world was turning towards extroversion. The Swamis and Yogis continue their practices, but only out of habit and without producing results. By contrast, something like the technical wonder of photography is today more likely to excite the Indians and awaken more powerful psychic forces in them than would the appearance of the god Vishnu in flesh and blood. Meanwhile in the West, the techniques of archaic magic are beginning to fascinate the white man who has been desiccated by technology. The psychic forces released are now capable of moving him and changing his whole life, and thus the pendulum has changed position.

Professor Toynbee listened to me with that extraordinary kindness that characterizes him, and remained sitting opposite me in silence, with the blue light of an Indian summer day playing over his white head. I am not sure that he shared my thoughts, and indeed, I was allowing them to rush forth without really feeling myself responsible for them. In a sense I was following the technique of Hindu thinking which Jung had explained to me.

We then talked of Jung, and Toynbee said that he had been in Zürich to take part in the celebration of Jung's birthday, and had given a talk about him on the radio. He had not seen him, however.

Afterwards, we leafed through one of Jung's books which is concerned with world problems, *The Undiscovered Self*. And we read some of its pages aloud sitting beneath a mango tree.

New Delhi
February 24, 1960

Dear Dr. Jung,

I was lunching with Professor Arnold Toynbee yesterday at my house, and he told me that he had recently been in Switzerland on your birthday. I'm sorry I did not know about it in order to greet you in time. Anyhow, please accept my warm congratulations and best wishes.

I am now reading your book, *The Undiscovered Self*. I talked to Toynbee about it. He gave some interesting lectures here in Delhi on 'A World Civilization', 'A World Religion', and so on. Following your ideas, I told Toynbee that it would probably be better for the Westerners to recede·into the background now and leave others to do the world's business, since the most urgent task for the Christian world today is to try to preserve Individuality, the *persona*, which is as delicate as a rose and which is in danger of perishing. I told him that mass and quantity have to be balanced by real quality, and that that could only come about through a revitalization of symbols—and that, I said, must be a quiet task.

Today I think you are the only light in this work. That will probably be realized better in the future, but I am not quite sure. There are also some artists who are now working with symbols who are trying to do this job, but I think they do so unconsciously.

Küsnacht-Zürich
Seestrasse 228,
March 31, 1960

Dear Mr. Serrano,

Thank you for your interesting letter. I quite agree with you that those people in our world who have insight and good will enough, should concern themselves with their own 'souls', more than with preaching to the masses or trying to find out the best way for them. They only do that, because they don't know themselves. But alas, it is a sad truth that usually those who know nothing for themselves take to teaching others, in spite of the fact that they know the best method of education is the good example.

Surely modern art is trying its best to make man acquainted with a world full of darkness, but alas, the artists themselves are unconscious of what they are doing.

The very thought that mankind ought to make a step forward and extend and refine consciousness of the human being, seems to be so difficult that nobody can understand it, or so abhorrent that nobody can take up his courage. All steps forward in the improvement of the human psyche have been paid for by blood.

I am filled with sorrow and fear when I think of the means of self-destruction which are heaped up by the important powers of the world. Meanwhile everybody teaches everybody, and nobody seems to realize the necessity that the way to improvement begins right in himself. If is almost too simple a truth. Everybody is on the lookout for organizations and techniques, where one can follow the other and where things can be done safely in company.

I would like to ask Mr. Toynbee: Where is your civilization and what is your religion? What he says to the masses will remain—I am afraid—sterile, unless it has become true and real in himself. Mere words have lost their spell to an extraordinary extent. They have been twisted and misused for too long a time.

I am looking forward to your new book with great interest! Hoping you are always in good health, I remain

Yours sincerely,

C. G JUNG.

I answered this important letter from Dr. Jung with a rather extensive one of my own, which in turn yielded me a reply of more than ten hand-written pages. Because it was written only a few months before his death, and because of its deep seriousness, it is for me something like his ideological testament and for that reason I will reproduce both of these letters in their entirety a little further along.

I Receive the Last Letter
from Dr. Jung

IN SEPTEMBER, 1960, I had to go to Chile and therefore passed through Zürich in hopes of seeing Professor Jung again. Mrs. Aniela Jaffe told me, however, that he was quite ill and in bed, and that therefore I could not visit him. She also told me that on the day before Jung had been working on his answer to my letter which was as yet unfinished. She advised me to take it as it was, and said that she would have him sign it in bed. She then asked me to call on her in her apartment on the following afternoon so that she could give me the letter.

I spent most of the day wandering through the old streets of Zürich, and ate lunch in a restaurant beside the cathedral. This cathedral has a monumental clock and an immense tree growing in the cloister. This tree seemed to represent the whole force of history; and in its antiquity it seemed to be the product of archaic forces and subterranean myths. Nearby was a low balcony which in the springtime blossomed with flowers, but which was now dry and forsaken in the winter snows.

The poet Goethe had lived in the neighbourhood, and a

dean of the cathedral, Johann Kaspar Lavater, who died in 1801, was his friend. Goethe had first visited the place in 1779. From his young manhood, Jung had always felt a great affinity with Goethe, and there was even a family legend which claims that the two are related through one of Goethe's natural sons.

I stood there quietly contemplating the clock tower, the low balcony and the tiny square. No one else was there, and it seemed as though time had stopped. Then a cat appeared and walked slowly and deliberately towards the balcony; it then stopped and lay down beneath it. A few moments later, I heard the sound of footsteps and a man emerged from one of the narrow streets and came into the square; his presence there seemed to increase the stasis of the scene, and he stood out alone against his surroundings, seemingly isolated from them.

As I stood there, I remembered another sight in the ancient city of Patan, near Katmandu in Nepal, where there is also a square. The pagodas and palaces which enclose it have curved roofs which stand out against the blue sky and the snows of the Himalayas in the distance. The square is decorated with golden statues, and the buildings are covered with wood carvings representing scenes of love. When I was there, the courtyards and the narrow streets which led into the square were heaped high with yellow grain drying in the sun. Then suddenly, a woman covered with a black shawl came into the square from one of the narrow lanes. She was wailing inconsolably, and her cries echoed across the clear morning air.

The difference between the two scenes was that the woman of Patan was a part of the landscape. Despite her tumultuous weeping, she seemed not to exist, but to be part of the collective mind. She belonged to the tradition, was connected to the hot soul of myth and to the blood of her gods. By contrast, the scene in the old square of Zürich was one of complete desolation. The man, with his hands in his overcoat pockets, was disconnected from everything, standing apart from his own landscape. He was the very image of the forlorn; he represented the *persona* and its fear of death. He was like a scrap from a morning newspaper which by noon was already out of date.

Nevertheless, there was an undeniable beauty in the European scene. It formed a delicate but profound pattern: the cathedral in the square, the balcony, the cat and the man. This was the dramatic beauty of individuality, mortality and the yearning for eternity.

That night I met some of Jung's disciples, and together we consulted the old horoscope of China, *I Ching*, which is also known as *The Book of Changes*. As I have already said, this book was introduced to the West by Richard Wilhelm and has since been incorporated into the living culture of modern man through the Jungian method. Jung had proposed the law of synchronicity, in which he hypothesized a correspondence between the world of objective reality and the soul of man, suggesting that each influenced and modified the other. In moments of great tension, when love or hate reaches an intense pitch, the soul influences external reality, and succeeds, so to speak, in 'changing the course of the stars'. Jesus said, 'Faith moves mountains,' and Oscar Wilde said, 'Nature imitates Art.' In the same synchronistic fashion, the stars influence the destiny of man and control the 'changes'. In more profound terms, destiny resides in the Unconscious, for the Unconscious is the mother of everything, perhaps even including the sky and all the constellations. The ancient Roman who 'unconsciously' tripped while leaving his house, used to go back inside, leaving the day's work undone. This is but one example of Synchronism, a concept which Jung has discussed in a book called *The Interpretation of Nature and the Psyche* which was written in collaboration with W. Pauli.

We perceive the external world through our senses, and what we cannot see, such as protons, electrons, and atoms, we conceive in the mind. That is to say, these perceptions are guessed at or—why not say it?—*invented*. When that happens, reality conforms precisely to a mental conception. Thus the *inconceivable* vitality, such as the atomic bomb, becomes not only *conceivable* but perceptible through mental processes, and we can justly say that the atomic explosion itself was essentially an idea.

The true nature of reality is quite beyond our comprehension, even when we use the most complicated technical instruments. For the person who builds these instruments and uses them, has in fact created them in the likeness of his ultimate instrument, his terrestrial mind. Thus all theory, all conception is only a working hypothesis, and ultimate reality will always remain inaccessible to us. What in any case counts, in the sciences as in everything else, is archetypal reality, which belongs to the soul and which, in a given moment in history, is imposed upon and gives form to that inaccessible reality. This archetypal reality is frequently arrived at from opposite directions and from people using quite different working hypotheses. Thus the atom bomb may be considered an archetypal reality, and also the Number Three which appears today in the communist trinity of Marx, Engels, and Lenin, just as it did in the past in the Father, Son and Holy Ghost, and in Brahma, Vishnu and Siva.

It is for this reason that Magic has never lost its force since it provides a means of dealing with 'reality'. It exists because of the correspondence which is to be found between 'reality' and the soul, as is indicated in the law of Synchronism. Thus when the soul is in a state of extreme tension, as for example in love, it creates miraculous forces actually capable of inducing transformation or transfiguration.

We sat on the floor of the hotel room and consulted the ancient book. The *I Ching* must only be used when all other methods fail; it is for extreme cases only. Since that then was my own condition, I was consulting it to find out whether the time had come for me to leave India. And the answer of the *I Ching* was: 'In order not to inhibit myself, I ought to dare the intersection of the great waters.'

Once again the *Book of Changes* had revealed its wisdom. I had to leave India in order to give balance to my soul, so that one day I could see with the necessary perspective the 'reality' of the Orient which I had created for myself.

Aniela Jaffe is a slender and graceful person, with a sensitive face and hands. We talked at great length, and the atmosphere of her small apartment was such that I let myself go, almost without thinking. Her apartment overlooked the courtyard of a convent, and from time to time the nuns would pass by, taking a stroll. Aniela Jaffe had come to be for Jung what Eckermann had been for Goethe. She saw to it that he finished his autobiography, which is a fundamental work that was published after his death, and which reveals many of the essential elements in his thought.

I was most grateful to Aniela Jaffe, because she had been an important link in the chain and had helped me meet Dr. Jung. That afternoon she gave me a document of incalculable value, ten manuscript pages by Professor Jung.

The Texts of the Letters

HERE NOW are the two letters. I include my own only because it motivated the last letter I received from Jung. It was written in English but was left unfinished because of his illness. At that time, the end was feared, but in fact Jung lived until June 7, 1961. He signed the letter on September 14, 1960, and as he had already said, he had put off writing it for more than a month.

My own letter is transcribed first:

New Delhi,
May 7, 1960

Dear Dr. Jung,

Your last letter was so important to me that I don't know how to thank you properly for it. Your words are so helpful and there is so much truth in what you say. Not everyone, however, will understand you. They will think that it is impossible to find solutions for actual problems if you isolate yourself and think only of perfecting yourself, and they will say: 'What about the masses?' and they will affirm that it is merely criminal egoism to pretend to perfect yourself in these circumstances.

But, in fact, it would seem that these people are ignorant of the true workings of the mind. For the mind is like a tape recorder or like a radio that receives and emits waves. I once remember having heard an interesting story. In it the angels asked God to destroy the world since mankind had reached the limits of evil. God then showed them a forgotten corner of the world where a young girl was praying. And God then said: 'For her alone I will not destroy the world.' Although this young girl did no more than pray, she managed to sustain the whole world. Thus it would seem that it is not the conscious mind that changes the world, but the unconscious. In a word, it is the Unconscious that changes the world. For this reason it is use-less to try and change or modify the Unconscious by using conscious means, by using reason or by doing things. The only way is to use ancient methods, like magic and alchemy, and to adopt the attitude of the ancients. Yet India, which has for long existed in this manner and used this method, has exhausted it, and no more results seem to be forthcoming. The same is true of the rest of the Orient. The West, on the other hand, appears to have exhausted the rational method and more insistence on it today will produce unhappiness for itself and for the rest of mankind.

Clearly a change is necessary. It was for this reason that I told Toynbee that the white man should now retire and let the others manage the affairs of the world. Just as there is no rational way of proving the immortality of the soul, so there is no rational way of countering the logic of Marxism or of historical materialism. Evidence for the immortality of the soul is found in other ways not dependent on reason. What is rationally certain today will no longer be certain tomorrow. The world is too unstable for reason. The Indians who clearly think thoughts that come from irrational sources now need something of the rationality of the West, and little by little they are beginning to learn it. The West, on the other hand, must learn to be illogical, for that is the only way to combat Com-munism, the growth of the power of the state and personal slavery. Still, the truth is that there are no absolute truths. All is merely creation. When Wilde said that nature imitates art, he was right in the sense that nature conforms to the unconscious will. From the lizard who changes his colours to the woman who adapts her physical body to the fashions of the time and the sense of beauty acceptable at a given moment, it is always the same. A faith, a strong belief, sustained and repeated, can give birth to reality. The Marxist ideas and laws of economic evolution are not really true, but if they are believed and repeated again and again without the opposition of a stronger and fundamentally different faith or belief, then they will come to be real simply because of the strong will which supports them. It is probable that there is no law of any kind in the world, and that all that exists is faith or the idea. That is what makes laws possible.

In principle, Toynbee is right when he states that history could be changed if man finds an appropriate reply to the challenge of the times, and when he affirms that it is necessary to use propaganda as a means of modifying the mind. He believes in the power of mind, but his mistake consists in the idea that the change can be produced consciously. The Communists will always do better with that. And in any case, the result would be devilish for the West and for the world at large, because we insist too much today on the same rational attitude, regardless of all other aspects and without natural compensation, without wholeness as you have said. The only way out of the impasse seems to be what you suggest: to revive symbols, to try to find the link that has been lost between science and alchemy or perhaps better, between science and the soul; because it is even possible that science itself may be a symbol —a projection. In its aspiration to conquer the Universe and its desire to explode the cosmos, science may again be expressing those old desires mankind has had to achieve totality or wholeness.

In any case, the Christian must look within himself and search in his own lacerated soul for some way of turning himself into a magician so that he will no longer use words, the *verbum*, sacrilegiously. For as you yourself have said, the word has lost its spell today. The word no longer creates worlds; words are nothing now. For this reason, the magician must not speak except in gestures. He must think thoughts from the Unconscious that are capable of tranforming the world. This is a most difficult task, and as you said, no one today has the strength or courage to undertake it. It is indeed so difficult, that man seems to prefer to go to other planets or to fly about in the sky—or even blow up the world. For those things are much easier to accomplish.

It is a tremendously difficult task trying to attain totality or wholeness. For many years I have felt that speaking and writing accomplish nothing; they merely create diffusiveness. Activity is contrary to being. Even so, I keep on writing.

Krishna Murti has said that there is no use following a master or Guru, or trying to reform the world. The only thing to do, he says, is to be quiet. Yet he continues to give lectures all over the world. Once I asked him why he bothered to talk, and he answering by saying: 'I do so for the same reason that a flower gives forth perfume. The flower doesn't know why it does it, but it is its natural expression.' I then asked him whether he liked talking so much, and he answered that he didn't because it tired him. One wonders whether the flower also becomes tired from giving forth perfume.

Everything about us today seems evil, and some things extremely so. Are these signs of the Apocalypse? Are the Hindu sages right when they speak of the theory of 'Kalpas'? Are we on the verge of another flood like the one that submerged Atlantis? The sower has sown his seed, and fixed and predetermined number have come forth. The rest don't matter; the world is now ploughed and will remain quiet until the next great sowing.

The difficult road the Christian now must take has been pointed out by you—or, one might say, rediscovered by you. How difficult it must have been to discover it! Doubtless that was why Hermann Hesse said that you were a gigantic mountain. Nevertheless, I don't believe that many understand you—not even your own disciples.

I remember that when I asked you in Locarno about the *chakras*, you said that they were 'centres of consciousness'; and then you gave me their Sanskrit names. But a little while later, when I was talking with Dr. Jacobi about the same thing, she said that *chakras* were not centres of consciousness but only of energy. Nevertheless, I know that you were right, for from my own experience I have discovered in my own body what might be called distinct zones of consciousness. Sometimes in the early morning, I have a feeling that my dreams come from different parts of my body. Some come from my knees, for example, and even after I wake up I can still feel them. If I don't interrupt them with rational thoughts, they continue to vibrate, and the images proceeding from my knees, or rather preserved there, flow up like a river towards my consciousness, or towards the light of day. Other truths like these can come from the heart or the belly. It is because of these things that I think a total being, totally conscious in all of its *chakras*, must be round, like the *being* of the alchemists, or like the stars and planets.

It is all a question of learning how to listen, because there are zones in us which know much more than we think they do. My knees, for example, know more, or at least quite different things, from what my head knows. Perhaps then in the act of listening we can arrive at that mysterious centre, which as you have said, appears to have no existence at all and seems to be something invented by ourselves; but which, nevertheless, actually surrounds and dominates us—to the extent that without it we are nothing. Without it, we are the dead burying the dead. In a way, that mysterious centre is our son, but at the same time it is our father. The Son who is the Father. The Self.

I wonder whether you can tell me, Dr. Jung, whether in your long experience you have ever met someone who has reached the Self by a technique, even by your technique, so that he was able to transform himself and change the centre of his consciousness? Personally, I am rather inclined to believe that it is not possible, but rather that it is something inborn. Some people seem to have this natural gift. I don't know why and nobody knows why, but people are born quite different. On the other hand, there may exist some sort of revelation. But even that seems to be less powerful than the inborn gift. Possibly this natural selection has something to do with what the Indians call *Karma* and reincarnation. It is even possible that your work, and mine, will only yield fruit in someone who is yet to be born. The work of today is harvested tomorrow. And it is also possible that that person who is to be born somewhere in the future will also be one of us again. Even so, since time is an illusion, our work produces instantaneous results.

With my best regards,
Miguel Serrano

Here now is the text of Dr. Jung's reply:

Küsnacht-Zürich,
Seestrasse 228,
September 14, 1960

Dear Mr. Serrano,

Your letter of May 7th, 1960 is so vast that I don't know where to begin answering it. The way towards a solution of our contemporary problems I seem to propose, is in reality the process I have been forced into as a modern individual confronted with the social, moral, intellectual and religious insufficiencies of our time. I recognize the fact that I can give only one answer, namely mine, which is certainly not valid universally, but may be sufficient for a restricted number of contemporary individuals. Inasmuch as my main tenet contains nothing more than: Follow that will and that way which experience confirms to be your own, i.e. the true expression of your individuality. As nobody can become aware of his individuality unless he is closely and responsibly related to his fellow beings, he is not withdrawing to an egoistic desert when he tries to find himself. He only can discover himself when he is deeply and unconditionally related to some, and generally related to a great many, individuals with whom he has a chance to compare, and from whom he is able to discriminate himself. If somebody in supreme egoism should withdraw to the solitude of Mt. Everest, he would discover a good deal about the amenities of his lofty abode, but as good as nothing about himself, i.e. nothing he could not have known before. Man in general is in such a situation, in so far as he is an animal gifted with self-reflection, but without the possibility of comparing himself to another species of animal equally equipped with consciousness. He is a top animal exiled on a tiny speck of planet in the Milky Way. That is the reason why he does not know himself; he is cosmically isolated. He only can state with certainty that he is no monkey, no bird, no fish and no tree. But what he positively is, remains obscure. Mankind of to-day is dreaming of interstellar communications. Could we contact the population of another star, we might find a means of learning something essential about ourselves. Incidentally we are just living in a time when *homo hominibus lupus* threatens to become an awful reality, and when we are in dire need to know beyond ourselves. The science fiction about travelling to the moon or to Venus and Mars and the lore about Flying Saucers are effects of our dim, but nonetheless intense need to reach a new physical as well as spiritual basis beyond our actual conscious world. Philosophers and pschologists of the XIXth and XXth Century have tried to provide a *terra nova* in ourselves, that is the *Unconscious*. This is indeed a discovery, which could give us a new orientation in many respects. Whereas our fictions about Martians and Venusians are based upon nothing but mere speculations, the Unconscious is within the reach of human experience. It is almost tangible and thus more or less familiar to us, but on the other hand, a strange existence difficult to understand. If we may assume that what I call the archetype is a verifiable hypothesis, then we are confronted with autonomous animals gifted with a sort of conciousness and a psychic life of their own, which we can observe, at least partially, not only in living men, but also in the historic course of many centuries. Whether we call them Gods, Demons or Illusions, they exist and function and are born anew with every generation. They have an enormous influence on individual as well as collective life and despite their familiarity, they are curiously non-human. This latter characteristic is the reason why they were called Gods and Demons in the past and why they are understood in our 'scientific' age as the psychical manifestations of the instincts, in as much as they represent habitual and universally occurring attitudes and thought forms. They are the basic forms, but not the manifest, personified or otherwise concretized images. They have a high degree of autonomy, which does not disappear, when the manifest images change. When, for instance, the belief in the god Wotan vanished and nobody thought of him anymore, the phenomenon originally called Wotan remained; nothing changed but its name, as National Socialism has demonstrated on a grand scale. A collective movement consists of millions of individuals, each of whom shows the symptoms of Wotanism and proves thereby that Wotan in reality never died, but has retained his original vitality and autonomy. Our consciousness only imagines that it has lost its Gods; in reality they are still there and it only needs a certain general condition in order to bring them back in full force. This condition is a situation in which a new orientation and adaptation is needed. If this question is not clearly understood and no proper answer given, the archetype, which expresses this situation, steps in and brings back the reaction, which has always characterized such times, in this case Wotan. As only certain individuals are capable of listening and of accepting good advice, it is most unlikely that anybody would pay attention to the statement of a warning voice that Wotan is here again. They would rather fall headlong into the trap.

As we have largely lost our Gods and the actual condition of our religion does not offer an efficacious answer to the world situation in general and to the 'religion' of communism in particular, we are very much in the same predicament as the pre-National-Socialistic Germany of the Twenties, i.e. we are apt to undergo the risk of a further, but this time worldwide, Wotanistic experiment. This means mental epidemy and war.

One does not realize yet, that when an archetype is unconsciously constellated and not consciously understood, one is *possessed by it* and forced to its fatal goal. Wotan then represents and formulates our ultimate principle of behaviour, but this obviously does not solve our problem.

The fact that an archaic God formulates and expresses the dominant of our behaviour means that we ought to find a new religious attitude, a new realization of our dependance upon

85

superior dominants. I don't know how this could be possible without a renewed self-understanding of man, which unavoidably has to begin with the individual. We have the means to compare Man with other psychical animalia and to give him a new definition. We can see him in a new setting which throws an objective light upon his existence, namely as a being operated and manoevred by archetypal forces instead of his 'free will', that is, his arbitrary egoism and his limited consciousness. He should learn that he is not the master in his own house and that he should carefully study the other side of his psychical world, which seems to be the true ruler of his fate.

I know this is merely a 'pious wish', the fulfilment of which demands centuries, but in each aeon there are at least a few individuals who understand what Man's real task consists of, and keep its tradition for future generations and a time when insight has reached a deeper and more general level. First the way of a few will be changed and in a few generations there will be more. It is most unlikely that the general mind within this or even in the next generation will undergo a noticeable change, as present man seems to be quite incapable of realizing that under a certain aspect he is a stranger to himself. But whoever is capable of such insight, no matter how isolated he is, should be aware of the law of sychronicity. As the old Chinese saying goes: 'The right man sitting in his house and thinking the right thought will be heard a hundred miles distant.'

Neither propaganda nor exhibitionist confessions are needed. If the archetype, which is universal, i.e. identical with itself always and anywhere, is properly dealt with in one place only it is influenced as a whole, i.e. simultaneously and everywhere. Thus an old alchemist gave the following consolation to one of his disciples: 'No matter how isolated you are and how lonely you feel, if you do your work truly and conscientiously, unknown friends will come and seek you.'

It seems to me that nothing essential has ever been lost, because its matrix is ever present with us and from this it can and will be reproduced if needed. But those can recover it who have learned the art of averting their eyes from the blinding light of current opinions and close their ears to the noise of ephemeral slogans.

You rightly say with Multatuli, the Dutch Philosopher: 'Nothing is quite true' and should add with him: 'And even this is not quite true.' The intellect can make its profound statement, that there is no absolute Truth. But if somebody loses his money, his money is lost and this is as good as an absolute Truth, which means that he will not be consoled by the intellectual profundity. There is a thing like convincing Truth, but we have lost sight of it, owing mostly to our gambling intellect, to which we sacrifice our moral certainty and gain thereby nothing but an inferiority-complex, which—by the way—characterizes Western politics.

To be is to do and to make. But as our existence does not depend solely upon our Ego-will, thus our doing and making depends largely upon the dominant of the unconscious. I am not only willing out of my Ego, but I am also made to be creative and active. To be quiet is only good for someone who has been too or perversely active. Otherwise it is an unnatural artifice, which unnecessarily interferes with our nature. We grow up, we blossom and we wilt; and death is ultimate quietude—or so it seems. But much depends upon the spirit, i.e. the meaning or significance, in which we do and make or—with another word— we live. This spirit expresses itself or manifests itself in a Truth, which is indubitably and absolutely convincing to the whole of my being in spite of the fact that the intellect in its endless ramblings will continue forever with its 'But, ifs', which how- ever should not be suppressed, but rather welcomed as occa- sions to improve your Truth.

You have chosen two good representants of East and West. Krishna Murti is all irrational, leaving solutions to quietude, i.e. to themselves as a part of Mother Nature. Toynbee on the other side believes in making and moulding opinions. None believes in the blossoming and unfolding of the individual as the experimental, doubtful and bewildering work of the living God, to whom we have to lend our eyes and ears and our discriminat- ing mind, to which end they have been incubated upon for millions of years and brought to light since about 6000 years ago, viz. at the moment when historical continuity of con- sciousness became visible through the invention of script.

We are sorely in need of a Truth or a self-understanding similar to that of Ancient Egypt, which I have found still living with the Taos Pueblos. Their chief of ceremonies, old Ochwiay Biano (Mountain Lake) said to me: 'We are the people who live on the roof of the world, we are the sons of the Sun, who is our father. We help him daily to rise and to cross over the sky. We do this not only for ourselves, but for the Americans also. Therefore they should not interfere with our religion. But if they continue to do so (by missionaries) and hinder us, then they will see that in ten years the sun will rise no more.'

He correctly assumes that their day, their light, their consciousness and their meaning will die, when destroyed through the narrowmindedness of American Rationalism, and the same will happen to the whole world, when subjected to such treatment. That is the reason why I tried to find the best truth and the clearest light I could attain to, and since I have reached my highest point and can't transcend any more, I am guarding my light and my treasure, convinced that nobody would gain and I myself would be badly, even hopelessly injured, if I should lose it. It is most precious not only to me, but above all to the darkness of the creator, who needs Man to illuminate his creation. If God had foreseen his world, it would be a mere senseless machine and Man's existence a useless freak.

My intellect can envisage the latter possiblity, but the whole of my being says 'No' to it.

Sincerely yours,

C. G. JUNG

A New Encounter

ON JANUARY 23, 1961, I once again returned to see Dr. Jung and talked with him in his study, where he sat surrounded by his books and works of art. As before, he had a pipe in his hand. 'This is a Swiss invention,' he said. 'It contains a well for water.'

'Rather like a hookah,' I said. Jung smiled and I then told him that I was going to leave India. 'I have consulted the *I Ching*, and it has advised me to do so.'

'You must do what it says,' he observed, 'because that book does not make mistakes. In any case, there is a definite connection between the individual psyche and the world. When I find it difficult for me to classify a patient, I always send him off to have a horoscope made. This horoscope always corresponds to his character, and I interpret it psychologically. So strong is the correspondence between the world and the psyche, that it is even possible that inventions and the ideas of three-dimensional time are simply reflections of the mental structure. Thus I was able to predict the last war simply from analysing my patients' dreams, because Wotan always used to appear in them. I was not able to predict the first World War however, because even though I had premonitions myself, I was not analysing dreams in those days. Altogether, I have analysed forty-one dreams which forecast grave illness or death.'

I kept my eyes on Dr. Jung as he spoke. As usual, he was lively and full of energy; and his eyes were at once humorous and and penetrating. Once again I noticed the jewelled ring on his finger. When making a point, he would lean forward for emphasis, and then would relax against the back of his chair, so that his movement was like that of a pendulum.

Much of my time in India I had spent trying to investigate the existence of what the Samkhya philosophers call the *Linga-Sarira*—or what the theosophists refer to as the Astral Body. I'd told Dr. Jung about these experiences in a letter to him, and had said that in my dreams I sensed the existence of a separate body within my own, which was capable of creating its own images. I had also talked to Aldous Huxley about this when he came through Delhi. He told me that he had been with D. H. Lawrence at the moment of his death, and said that it had been an extraordinary experience. Lawrence told him that he could feel himself coming out of his own body, as though he were standing in a corner of the room looking at himself lying in bed. I had also talked to the Dalai Lama about these strange experiences. I once asked him if he believed whether a voluntary detachment of the Astral Body was possible, and he answered me in this way: 'Yes, it is possible—during meditation. The texts describe three periods in this process: first, objective concentration on the self; second, a partial dissociation of the mind when, while perceiving the self, it is at once a part of it and not a part of it; and third, a condition in which the individual is no longer a part of that self, or rather has penetrated through it, which amounts to the same thing. . . .'

I told Dr. Jung about these conversations, and he said, "All these experiences are subjective, and are not collectively verifiable. Possibly one could attribute them to the Collective Unconscious. Nevertheless, it would be wrong to negate the possibility of the *Linga-Sarira* as an hypothesis. For I have seen mediums moving objects at a distance.'

I then asked him if he had known Gustav Meyrink. 'He

describes extremely interesting experiences in his books,' I said.

'I never met him, but I have read his works and consider them important. There are profound truths in *The Green Face (Das Grüne Gesicht)*.'

'Years ago I had an experience I want to tell you about,' I said. 'When I was a very young boy, I used to have the feeling at night, that I was dividing, or splitting away from myself. These feelings were always preceded by vibrations which rose along the length of my body, starting from the soles of my feet. These vibrations varied in intensity, but in the end they grew so powerful that I was afraid I was going to die. I remember once in particular when the vibration became virtually unendurable; and then suddenly, right in front of me a basin appeared. As though commanded to do so, I thrust my hands into the basin and then spread the strange liquid it contained all over my body. Immediately the vibrations ceased. All this took place in a state which was by no means dreamlike; it was entirely real—indeed, on a plane of reality far higher than that of ordinary perception. But I was never able to retain that degree of reality when, so to speak, I returned to my own body and found myself lying in bed. For years, I tried to produce those same phenomena voluntarily.

Dr. Jung then made this observation: 'As I said, those are all subjective experiences, and they are not collectively verifiable. What you call vibrations may only have been dreams, or at most, manifestations of the Collective Unconscious.'

I was disappointed by Jung's answer. He seemed incapable of penetrating these mysteries, and for a sad moment, I had the feeling that all he had done in his work was to create a new terminology to explain old truths. I had been similarly disappointed by the Dalai Lama, who had made no revealing statements about my phenomena, but had relied on ancient dogma, citing texts in support of his observations. Perhaps he had been afraid of exceeding himself as the head of a church, and in the presence of his court officials. It is always a heavy task to be responsible for a body of organized religious doctrine —or for a school of scientific psychology.

I then realized that I would never find any guidance, or explanation, for my personal experiences—which for Jung, were purely subjective—and I knew that I would have to rely solely upon my own intuition. I would have to walk alone, as Jung himself had once done, along the 'razor's edge'.

'It's very pleasant to talk about all this with someone who is not a patient,' Jung said.

'I've also come to see Hermann Hesse,' I said. 'We have also spoken many times about Yoga. He believes that the right road is simply one which is in agreement with nature.'

'That is also my philosophy,' said Jung. 'Man should live according to his own nature; he should concentrate on self-knowledge and then live in accordance with the truth about himself. What would you say about a tiger who was a vegetarian? You would say, of course, that he was a bad tiger. Thus everyone must live in accordance with his nature, both individually and collectively. The best example of that method is to be found in India, and the worst, I suppose, is in Russia. Russia is a country with a magnificent organization, but it doesn't function at all, as is obvious in its agricultural failures. The Russians haven't bothered to discover what man really is; they have simply tried to treat him as a wholly rational and mechanical being. Obviously what is necessary for them is not to devise a theory about agriculture, but to devise a theory about man, and to impose that theory or concept. I once knew an old lady who was very aristocratic and noble, and who conducted her life according to the most exquisite ideas of refinement; but at night she would dream about drunkenness, and in those dreams she herself would become hopelessly intoxicated. And so one must be what one is; one must discover one's own individuality, that centre of personality, which is equidistant between the conscious and the unconscious; we must aim for that ideal point towards which nature appears to be directing us. Only from that point can one satisfy one's needs.'

Dr. Jung then paused, and after a moment I said, 'The Hindus would seem to be saying the same thing when they say that it is better to be partially fulfilled within one's own *karma*, than perfectly within a foreign *karma*.'

'Exactly.'

'Professor Jung,' I asked, 'do you believe that your system could function outside of the West, that is where the psyche is not so divided? For example, there are no neurotics in India, and so far as I know, there are none in Burma, or in Indonesia, Thailand or China. And I suppose the reason is that the inhabitants of those countries are not persons in the Western Christian sense. As you said, when we first talked in Locarno, the *persona* is the product of the sudden imposition of Christianity upon a barbarous Nordic people, with all its resultant inhibitions and uncontrollable drives.'

'Yes,' said Jung quietly and reflectively, 'and I suppose that very lack of personality is what makes the East able to accept with such ease collective systems like Communism, and religious systems like Buddhism, which aim above all to annihilate the idea of personality. . . .'

As before, the time has passed rapidly and unnoticed. But I could see the afternoon shadows falling outside of the window, and I was afraid of tiring him. Before leaving, however, I wanted to say one more thing:

'A little while ago, when I was lunching with Hesse, I asked him how it was that I'd had the good fortune to find myself seated at his table; and he told me that it was no mere accident since only the right guests came there. He spoke of the Hermetic Circle.'

Jung smiled softly and said, 'That's true; mind attracts mind. Only the *correct* ones come, and we are directed by the Unconscious, because the Unconscious knows.'

But as I listened, I began to wonder. What exactly is the Unconscious of which Jung spoke so familiarly? Meyrink used to say: 'If the Mother of God is in the Unconscious, then the Unconscious is the Mother of God. . . .'

But Jung continued to talk: 'Once I was on a train, and a General sat down beside me. We talked, and although he did not know who I was, he told me all about his dreams, which is certainly unusual for a man of his position. The General considered that his dreams were absurd, but after listening to him, I told him that one of his dreams had changed his whole life, and that otherwise he would have been an intellectual. The General was startled and looked at me as though I were a witch, or at least a person gifted with second sight. But in reality, it was the Unconscious which was knowing and directing. The General had sat down next to me because he was unconsciously searching for an answer.' Jung smiled, and a certain distant light came into his eyes. 'In the same way, I could tell you things about your own life which would startle you. . . .'

Jung then leaned forward and gazed fixedly into my eyes. In the shadows of the late afternoon, his body seemed to grow larger and larger, and I had the feeling that I was facing an incarnation of Abraxas. I felt a sudden chill, and then seemed to hear distant voices coming from this powerful being, swirling about us both, like echoes out of the ages.

The Seven Sermons of the Dead

IN 1925, Jung published a strange book in a limited edition. This publication was anonymous, and it was only after his death, with the printing of his memoirs, that his authorship of the book was acknowledged openly. It was apparently an exercise in automatic writing, written as though dictated from the 'other world' or, as he would say, from the Collective Unconscious. The 'person' who dictated it to him was an archetype, a kind of Master or Wise Man. From the time of that first encounter with this Archetype of the Soul, Jung lived under the strain and agony of the relationship. He struggled against listening to these strange voices, but at the same time he surrendered to them.

Jung gave the name of Philemon to this ancient wise man who appeared before him, revealing the secrets that lay in the depths of his own soul. Jung finally succeeded in sketching him, and he appears in silhouette form in the Red Book which Jung wrote at that time, more or less as a diary. In this way, Philemon became equated with the Ancient of the Days, the Walker of the Dawn, the Master and the Guru who speaks from beyond time and beyond dimension.

In India, as indeed in Chile, I have met other men who say that they receive their orders and their whole moral structure from beings who inhabit another world. These supernatural beings never take on fleshly form even though they have been sketched and drawn in the same way that Jung produced his silhouette of Philemon.

Jung has told us how he came to write that strange book

which he originally titled in Latin, *VII Sermons Ad Mortuos*, which had been dictated to him by Philemon. Nevertheless, when it was published, he attributed it to Basilides, a Gnostic of Alexandria, 'the City where the East toucheth the West'.

The most extraordinary things happened just before that book came to be written. Jung's house was filled with noise, the atmosphere was tense, and the rooms seemed to be filled with invisible presences. Both he and his sons had strange dreams, and they all felt that something like a personified Destiny had entered their daily lives to spy on them. All these experiences ceased the moment the book was finished.

The book itself is written in an archaic style which is slightly confusing, but which was probably inevitable in view of the noumenal impact of the Archetype. Many Jungians are opposed to the circulation of this book because they are afraid that it will damage the scientific reputation of its author, and confirm the accusation made by many of his critics that he was merely a mystic. But Jung himself already acknowledged it in his memoirs. In the German edition of this work, *The Seven Sermons of the Dead* are reproduced in their entirety, but the English translation is somewhat expurgated.

I myself did not come across the *Sermons* until after Jung's death, when I discovered them in London. That was the English private edition of 1925. In this extraordinary book Jung speaks of Abraxas in the following way:

There is a god whom ye knew not, for mankind forgot it. We name it by its name ABRAXAS. It is more indefinite still than god and devil. . . .Abraxas is effect. Nothing standeth opposed to it but the ineffective; hence its effective nature freely unfoldeth itself. The ineffective is not, therefore re-sisteth not. Abraxas standeth above the sun and above the devil. It is improbable probability, unreal reality. Had the pleroma a being, Abraxas would be its manifestation. It is the effective itself, not any particular effect, but effect in general.

It is unreal reality, because it hath no definite effect.

It is also creatura, because it is distinct from the Pleroma.

The sun hath a definite effect, and so hath the devil. Where-fore do they appear to us more effective than indefinite Abraxas.

It is force, duration, change. . . .

. . . Hard to know is the deity of Abraxas. Its power is the greatest, because man perceiveth it not. From the sun he draweth the *summun bonum*; from the devil the *infinum malum*: but from Abraxas LIFE, altogether indefinite, the mother of good and evil.

Smaller and weaker life seemeth to be than the summum bonum; wherefore is it also hard to conceive that Abraxas transcendeth even the sun in power, who is himself the radiant source of all the force of life.

Abraxas is the sun, and at the same time the eternally sucking gorge of the void, the belittling and dismembering devil.

The power of Abraxas is twofold; but ye see it not, because for your eyes the warring opposites of this power are extinguished.

What the god-sun speaketh is life.

What the devil speaketh is death.

But Abraxas speaketh that hallowed and accursed word which is life and death at the same time.

Abraxas begetteth truth and lying, good and evil, light and darkness, in the same word and in the same act. Wherefore is Abraxas terrible.

It is splendid as the lion in the instant he striketh down his victim.

It is beautiful as a day of spring.

It is the great Pan himself and also the small one.

It is Priapos.

It is the monster of the under-world, a thousand-armed polyp, coiled knot of winged serpents, frenzy.

It is the hermaphrodite of the earliest beginning.

It is the lord of the toads and frogs, which live in the water and go up on the land, whose chorus ascendeth at noon and at midnight.

It is the abundance that seeketh union with emptiness.

It is holy begetting.

It is love and love's murder.

It is the saint and his betrayer.

It is the brightest light of day and the darkest night of madness.

To look upon it, is blindness.

To know it, is sickness.

To worship it, is death.

To fear it, is wisdom.

To resist it not, is redemption.

God dwelleth behind the sun, the devil behind the night. What god bringeth forth out of light the devil sucketh into the night. But Abraxas is the world, its becoming and its passing. Upon every gift that cometh from the god-sun the devil layeth his curse.

Everything that ye entreat from the god-sun begetteth a deed of the devil.

Everything that ye create with the god-sun giveth effective power to the devil.

That is terrible Abraxas.

It is the mightiest creature, and in it the creature is afraid of itself.

It is the manifest opposition of creatura to the Pleroma and its nothingness.

It is the son's horror of the mother.

It is the mother's love for the son.

It is the delight of the earth and the cruelty of the heavens.

Before its countenance man becometh like stone.

Before it there is no question and no reply.

It is the life of creatura.

It is the operation of distinctiveness.

It is the love of man.

It is the speech of man.

It is the appearance and the shadow of man.

It is illusory reality.'

The Farewell

ON WEDNESDAY, MAY 10, 1961, I once again tried to see Jung. I felt some strange impulse forcing me to do so, and I was fearful of allowing too much time to go by. Jung died only twenty-seven days after my visit, and I believe that I was therefore the last foreign friend who saw him, or who had an important conversation with him.

Up until the last moment, I did not know whether I would be able to see him. Miss Ruth Bailey had told me on the telephone that she would see me and that we could have tea together, but she said that Jung was seriously ill and in bed. In any event, I went over to Küsnacht in the afternoon and met Miss Bailey. We sat in a little reception room on the ground floor, and I then asked her whether I might see something of the house. She showed me the dining-room with its Renaissance paintings and its antique furniture, and we then went into the living-room and sat down. Miss Bailey is an extraordinary woman: she had accompanied Jung on his expeditions to Africa, and looked after him during the last years of his life. She has a quick intelligence and an interesting face, enhanced by a certain elegance, although it was then clouded by anxiety. She made me think of Miraben, the English disciple of Mahatma Gandhi, who had been with him up to the end of his life. After that, Miraben settled in Greece, having decided that she couldn't bear India without Gandhi. As it was to turn out, Miss Bailey also left Switzerland after Jung died, and now lives in England doing social work for indigent mothers. There is something sad about the fate of these two women who had to continue on alone without the figures they so venerated.

During tea—that very English ritual—Miss Bailey told me that I was very lucky because Jung's health had markedly improved that morning, and he wanted to see me after we had had our tea. In the meantime, she talked about death, ruminating quietly. 'C. G. accuses me of keeping him here on earth,' she said. 'He says that he wants to leave, but that I prevent him. Nevertheless, I think he still wants to live, and certainly his sharp sense of humour is an indication of his vitality.'

'Do you think there is any existence after death?' I asked.

'Certainly,' she replied, 'I couldn't conceive of Jung being ended, just like that. . . .' Miss Bailly made the gesture of turning off a light switch. 'Moreover,' she continued, 'there are psychological proofs of the probability of an after-life. The Unconscious contains a sense of continuity and of survival beyond the threshold of death. It's as though the Unconscious simply ignored death and is not afraid of it. Jung tells me that he has had dreams about death, and that the visions are curiously familiar.'

Miss Bailey paused for a moment, and then continued:

'You know, Jung has been very busy these past few days writing an essay called "Man and His Symbols" for an American publication. The work has exhausted him, however. He writes it all by hand and has now completed eighty pages;

he is writing directly in English, because he is afraid that German syntax may confuse his meaning and hopes that it will be more clear in English '

As Miss Bailey gave me another cup of tea, she pronounced the same statement that Elsy Bodmer and Ninon Hesse had made: 'I think that there is a profound relationship between you and Jung. He is always very cheerful when he sees you, and he has looked forward to your coming today.'

She paused for a moment and then asked me whether I knew the Bollingen Tower. This tower had been built by Jung beside a lake in the country, near a place called Bollingen. He had built it by impulse, and its construction was determined by his dreams. The tower was Jung's attempt to express his idea of the Self in stone. Thus it represents his whole psychological system. In former years, Jung stayed there for weeks on end. He had a small boat and used to sail across the lake. He would build a fire for his own cooking, which he did himself, and he made no use of electricity. On the stone walls of his tower he had carved sentences from the Gnostics and the Egyptian alchemists; he had also outlined *mandalas* and other magic symbols. I told Miss Bailey that I had never seen it.

'It's very interesting,' she said, 'You should visit it. I have helped Jung perform some rites there. In the morning, when he came into his little kitchen, Jung would greet each one of his cooking utensils—the saucepans, pots, and frying pans. He told me I must also do so. "They understand and appreciate it," he said. Jung always used the same frying pan and pots because they were his friends, and he considered them old acquaintances with whom to chat in the solitude of his retreat. For Jung, all things are animated with their own life, or with the life he transmits to them.'

Tea finished, Miss Bailey suggested that I go up to see Jung. She asked me to keep the interview short, since she was afraid of tiring him. Thus for the last time, I climbed the stairs up to his room. She left me on the landing, and I went in alone.

Jung was seated beside the window, as he had been in our former meetings. On that day, however, he was dressed in a Japanese ceremonial gown, so that in the light of the late afternoon, he looked like a magician or a priest of some ancient cult. When I entered the room, Jung tried to rise from his chair, but I hurriedly prevented him from doing so. I then gave him the small gift which I had brought him from the East—a turquoise box from Kashmir similar to the one which I had given Hermann Hesse in Montagnola. He took it in his old hands, looking at it and feeling it, and said: 'Turquoise from Kashmir. I never went there; I only saw Bengal and the north-east of India, and Madura in the south. Thank you for this beautiful gift.'

I told him that I had just come from seeing Hermann Hesse, and that we had talked about death. I said that I had asked Hesse whether it was important to know if there was something beyond death. Hesse had said that he thought not, that he thought that death was probably like entering the Collective Unconscious, falling into it, perhaps. . . .'

'Your question was badly put,' Jung replied. 'It would be better phrased in this way: Is there any reason to believe that there is life after death?'

'And is there?' I asked.

'Were it possible for the mind to function at the margin of the brain, it would be incorruptible.'

'Is such a thing possible?'

'Parapsychological phenomena suggest that it is,' he said. 'I myself have experienced certain things which also indicate it. Once I was gravely ill, almost in a coma. Everybody thought that I was suffering terribly, but in fact, I was experiencing something extremely pleasant. I seemed to be floating over my body, far above it. Then, after my father died, I saw him several times. Of course that does not mean that he in fact appeared. His appearances may have been entirely subjective phenomena on my part.'

'But isn't it possible that all these things are in fact external and objective, and not merely something which happens in the mind?' I asked. 'Hesse talks about the Collective Unconscious as if it existed externally, and he considers that death may merely be a *falling into* that state.'

'During the War,' Jung said, 'I saw men who had received brain wounds which paralysed the functions of the cerebral cortex, and thus prevented them from having any sense of time or space. Nevertheless, they were still able to dream, and some of them had important visions. Now if the brain is entirely paralyzed, the question is what organ produces the dream? With what part of his body does a man dream? Is it something physical? Or is it an indication that in fact the mind acts independently of the brain? I don't know, but it's an interesting hypothesis.'

Jung paused for a moment before continuing. 'There are other phenomena which can support this hypothesis,' he said. 'You know, of course, that a small child has no clearly defined sense of the Ego. The child's ego is diffused and dispersed throughout his body. Nevertheless, it has been proven that small children have dreams in which the Ego is clearly defined, just as it is in mature people. In these dreams, the child has a clear sense of the *persona*. Now if, from a physiological point of view, the child has no Ego, what is it in the child which produces these dreams, dreams which, I may add, affect him for the rest of his life? And another question: If the physical Ego disappears at death, does that other Ego also disappear, that other which had sent him dreams as a child?'

As I listened to him, I was once again struck by the magnificent rigour of Jung's mind. On the very threshold of death he was still searching and hoping to believe; but his scientific objectivity prevented him from pronouncing a single word which would not correspond to demonstrable experiences.

'Today no one pays attention to what lies behind words,' he said, 'to the basic ideas that are there. Yet the idea is the only thing that is truly there. What I have done in my work, is simply to give new names to those ideas, to those realities. Consider, for example, the word "Unconscious". I have just finished reading a book by a Chinese Zen Buddhist. And it seemed to me that we were talking about the same thing, and that the only difference between us was that we gave different words to the same reality. Thus the use of the word Unconscious doesn't matter; what counts is the idea that lies behind the word.'

On the small table beside the chair where Jung was sitting, was a book called *The Human Phenomenon* by Teilhard de Chardin. I asked Jung whether he had read it.

'It is a great book,' he said. His face was pale, but seemed strangely illuminated by an inner light. His hands, protruding from the wide sleeves of the Oriental gown, were at once gnarled and delicate. Once again, I noticed the Gnostic ring on his finger, and asked him what the symbols meant.

'It is Egyptian,' he answered. 'Here the serpent is carved, which symbolizes Christ. Above it, the face of a woman; below the number 8, which is a symbol of the Infinite, of the Labyrinth, and of the Road to the Unconscious. I have changed one or two things on the ring so that the symbol will be Christian. All of these symbols are absolutely alive within me, and each one of them creates a reaction within my soul.'

I then told Jung that I thought that in his own being he represented a link with the secrets of the past. 'You have found the connecting road, the path which was lost with the coming of the European Enlightenment, if not before. Just as the Renaissance found a bond with the external Classic Age, so you, for our own time, seem to have established a link with its internal side. Thus, thanks to you, the essential qualities of man are able to survive. In his own time, Meister Eckhart performed the same role.'

'What I have tried to do,' he said, 'is to show the Christian what the Redeemer really is, and what the resurrection is. Nobody today seems to know, or to remember, but the idea still exists in dreams.'

I then told Jung that I had gone to Florence to see Leonardo's painting, 'The Annunciation'. And I told him that when I was looking at that picture, I thought of the Massacre of the Innocents, an event which coincided with, and in a real sense polarized, the birth of Christ. 'Much fuss has been made about the death of Christ,' I said, 'but no one bothers about the death of so many innocents. Their deaths seem to be accepted merely as something necessary for the birth of a Redeemer. It was the same with the birth of Krishna when all the children of the district born on that same day were ordered to be executed by the tyrant Kansa. Thus there always seems to me to be something terribly unjust about the coming of a Redeemer; indeed, one might almost consider it a positive evil. There is always the question of whether the end justifies the means.'

Jung remained silent for a while, and then said slowly, 'And to think that those who are sacrificed are often the best. . . .'

I then asked Jung whether he thought there was something essentially irrelevant in our discussion of such things, whether our concerns were really outdated in this present age of super-technology and interplanetary travel. I told him that I'd asked Hesse what he thought would happen to introspective people in the future, and that he had been very pessimistic.'

'Space flights to other worlds are still a long way off,' Jung answered. 'Sooner or later man will have to return to earth, and to the land from which he comes; that is to say, man will have to return to himself. Space flights are merely an escape, a fleeing away from oneself, because it is easier to go to Mars or to the moon than it is to penetrate one's own being. But what is dangerous about this frantic interest in spatial conquest is that it symbolizes a state of complete anxiety in man. This anxiety would seem to be caused by a fear of the world's population explosion. In a way, space flights seem to be an instinctive reaction to this problem.'

Jung was about to expand on this idea, but the door opened and Miss Bailey entered. I then realized that I had stayed too long. At the same time, I knew that this was to be my last meeting, and I sensed that Jung realized it as well. Miss Bailey said that Jung's daughter and her husband had come and that they were waiting below. She then left so that I could say good-bye.

I clasped his hands and bowed and then moved very slowly towards the door. When I reached it I turned back to look at him. He was contemplating me very fixedly, wrapped in the light of the late afternoon which played on his Oriental gown. He raised his hand and made a sign of farewell.

An Indian Morning

THAT DAY I rose very early. It was a midsummer's morning, and already the heat had begun to rise. I walked out on to the terrace beside my room and glanced at the mango tree which cast its shadows across the lawn. I greeted the sun and then began my Yoga exercises. After a little while, I saw the bearer in his turban walking barefoot along the path. When he reached me, he put his hands together and said, 'Namaste' which means, more or less, 'I greet the God who is within you.' He then handed me a telegram. I opened it immediately and read in the glare of the morning light, the following message: 'Professor Jung died peacefully yesterday.' It was signed 'Bailey and Jaffe'. The strong light of the sun and the heat then forced me to move.

That morning I had to go to the Delhi airport to say good-bye to Prime Minister Nehru who was leaving for a holiday in the Himalayas. He was going to the Kulu Valley, or the Valley of the Gods. When I reached the airport, Nehru was already walking towards the airplane. He was dressed in white, and his graceful figure moved elegantly, with that spiritual elegance which was always a part of his charm.

I showed him the telegram I had received a few hours earlier, for Nehru was also an admirer of Jung. I then said, 'You know how interested Jung was in India. A word of condolence from you or from your government would be deeply appreciated.'

Nehru meditated for a moment. 'From here, I can't manage to give the order personally,' he said. 'But please speak to Mr. Desai, the Secretary for Foreign Affairs, and ask him to send a telegram of condolence in my name.'

And so it was that India was present at the death of the man who had worked so hard to understand the profound values of its civilization, and to bring the values of India to bear on the Western world. And so, too, another Great Circle was closed.

I spent all that afternoon and the following day in meditation, trying to concentrate on the image of Jung, and trying to imagine what was happening to him now in his great journey of transmigration into the kingdom of shadows. I wondered whether he was undergoing those rites which he had tried to understand before and had described in his commentary to the *Tibetan Book of the Dead*. I then wrote Hermann Hesse the letter which he later had published in the special edition of *Neue Zürcher Zeitung* which was dedicated to Jung. I also wrote my condolences to Jung's family, to Miss Bailey and to Mrs. Jaffe.

Shortly afterwards I received a letter from Miss Bailey, in which she described the last moments of our friend:

Küsnacht, Zürich
June 16, 1961

Dear Mr. Serrano,

Thank you so much for your very kind letter which was a great comfort to me. Now my work—it was a very great privilege indeed to be able to look after 'C. G.'—is over, I feel very lost and desolate, but the kind letters from his friends help me so much in my loneliness, and the feeling of inability to face life without him.

He died so very peacefully, just went to sleep at the end, and he wanted to go. He was so very tired and weak. On May 17th, after a very happy and peaceful day before, he had an embolism, a blood clot in the brain and it affected his speech a little. You can imagine this was a great shock to me, it happened at breakfast time. But after a few days he began to pick up again and his speech improved very well, but he could not read so well and I spent much time reading to him. Then on May 30th, again after a very peaceful and happy day, we were sitting in the library window having tea when he had a collapse and that was the last time he was in the library, afterwards he was in his room. From this time onwards he got weaker and weaker, and for two days before he died he was away in some far country and he saw wonderful and beautiful things, I am sure of that. He smiled often and was happy. The last time we sat out on the terrace he told me of the wonderful dream he had had; he said: 'Now I know the truth but there is still a small piece not filled in and when I know that, I shall be dead.' Also after that he had a wonderful dream which he told me in the night. He saw a huge round block of stone sitting on a high plateau and at the foot of the stone was engraved these words: 'And this shall be a sign unto you of Wholeness and Oneness.' I should have known from this that his life was complete, all these last days I should have known that he was leaving me. I think I did know but pushed the knowledge aside, and perhaps that was merciful because I might not have been able to do what I had to do for him. I could stay with him night and day.

Dear Mr. Serrano, I cannot write much more now but I hope to see you again and I shall be clearer in my mind then perhaps, to tell you of many strange things. I am going to

England for a few weeks but I am to come back again and keep open the house and there is so much to be done yet, it will take months. The members of his family are very kind to me. The family received the message from Mr. Nehru and were deeply touch by it. 'C. G.' liked you so much and I feel my friendship with you is a valuable thing to me, I found it easy to talk with you always.

The turquoise box you brought for him he gave to me in these last days. Because of our mutual love and regard for him, I hope you don't mind that, or would you like it back again? Now no more.

Thank you again so much for your kind thoughts of me.

Yours very sincerely,
RUTH BAILEY

A Dream

ON OCTOBER 20, 1961, I was in the city of Mysore in South India, and at six o'clock in the morning, I had a dream about Professor Jung. I was walking with him along a dusty road. We were walking side by side, with our elbows almost touching. Two generations: he, the very old man, and I still young. Then a man came by who greeted us. Jung answered the greeting and I took off my wide-brimmed hat. Jung then spoke, and I was aware of his very great age. The walk had tired him, and he seemed exhausted. 'I am very old and tired,' he said. 'I have now lived my life and the time has come for me to die. To fight against it would cause tremendous suffering to the body, as I already know.'

I then realised that he was referring to his blood clot. I told him that his physical sufferings would be compensated for by wisdom, since he would know what death was like. He was perhaps the only one interested in knowing about death, in comparison to the hundreds of scientists who were working to discover what life is. And so I then turned to him and asked: 'What is death?'

And he answered, 'Death is *Li* and *Tata*.' I couldn't understand what he meant and told him so, and he therefore translated: 'Water and Stone.'

'I have spent eighty years trying to discover what was

behind water,' he said, 'and all that time I was in it. I have now passed through it, and in the end I have come out to the place where the horses run. . . .'

I looked down at a nearby irrigation ditch. Some water flowed past and then there was nothing. Jung continued to talk like an enlightened person, uttering sentences of extraordinary poetry. I heard them and wanted to retain them, but I knew I should forget them instantly, for they were words which could not be retained. They were like revelations: to be heard, wondered at, and forgotten.

After that experience, I was overwhelmed with a sense of desolation, and with a feeling that I had faced the mystery of death. I was afraid that Jung had returned from death to tell me that he had discovered nothing, and that there was nothing. On the other hand, perhaps he wanted to reveal that life continues outside of the Ego in the forces of nature, and in the language of poetry.

Jung Returns to Receive Me in his House

IN THE FIRST PART of this book, I have told how, after Hermann Hesse's death, I went with my eldest son to visit his widow. On that same occasion, coming down from Montagnola, I decided that I would also show him Jung's house.

We arrived at Küsnacht one afternoon, and walked into the park until we reached the gate with its Latin inscription. We rang the bell and waited. After a while, a young man of my son's age opened the door. He was one of Jung's grandchildren, and I explained to him who I was and what I wanted; but the young man said that since his parents were not at home, he could not let us enter. I was very disappointed and was about to leave, when a car came into the grounds and stopped near us. A woman got out who proved to be Jung's daughter, Mrs. Niehus-Jung, and she was the young man's aunt. When she recognized me, she asked us to come into the house immediately. She then told me that the house was occupied by her brother, an architect. 'Life continues to go on,' she said, 'and that would have made my father happy. But do you know, something very strange has just happened. I had no intention of coming here today; I was going somewhere else. But as I came along the road, I felt as though I was being forced or directed to stop here.'

It sounds odd, but I really believe that Jung was once again receiving me at his house; he was incapable of letting me stand at the door like a stranger. I took my son upstairs to the study and found that everything was almost the same. The shelves still contained his books, but his work table was gone, and something in the atmosphere had also changed. The painting showing Siva on top of Mount Kailas was still on the wall, however. I tried to recall our last meeting and our fare-well; and with half-closed eyes, I was almost able to see Dr. Jung sitting there beside the large window.

Mrs. Niehus-Jung told us that at her father's request, his valuable library of alchemical books would be open to the public. She then led us into the garden to show us something. I noticed that many old trees had recently been cut down in order to allow a view of the lake. She then led us to a tree which Jung used to sit under, and she showed us a huge scar that ran along the trunk from top to bottom.

'When my father died,' she said, 'there was a tremendous storm over Küsnacht—something which never happens at that time of year. And in the course of the storm, this tree was struck by lightning. He always used to sit in the shade here, you know.'

I looked at the long scar made by the heavenly fire, and I took it as a sign that Jung had reached the centre of universal forces. Nature had responded; it had been moved; there was *synchronicity*.

And so, if my dream had brought me anguish and doubt, I was now faced with other significant facts which seemed, at least externally, to equalize that nothingness. Or perhaps, I had simply misinterpreted the dream.

Standing there, I heard my son say, 'How beautiful it is here. I should like to live here forever.' He went down to the edge of the lake and let the waves play over his feet.

The Jung family tomb is in the graveyard at Küsnacht, and

we went there to visit it. Standing on the ground is a large
round stone with a cavity in the centre which catches rain-
water. Nearby is another vertical stone engraved with the
family crest. The base of this stone is squared, and on each
side is a Latin inscription:

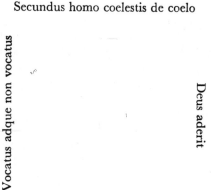

Secundus homo coelestis de coelo

Vocatus adque non vocatus

Deus aderit

Primus homo terrenus de terra

'First, the terrestrial man of the earth,' 'Second, the celestial
man of heaven.' I believe these are taken from the writings of
St. Paul. The other part of the inscription is of course the
same as is found on the gate of Jung's house: 'Called or not
called, God is present.'

A Myth for Our Time

AT THE END of his letter of September 14, 1960, Jung has
written: 'I am guarding my light and my treasure, convinced
that nobody would gain and I myself would be badly, even
hopelessly injured, if I should lose it. It is most precious not
only to me, but above all to the darkness of the Creator, who
needs Man to illuminate his Creation.'

This thought is elaborated in Jung's posthumous memoirs
and is illustrated by his story of the chief of the Pueblo Indians,

Ochwiay Biano, who believed he was helping the sun to rise at dawn. Jung had tried to find for modern man a myth as transcendent and vital as that one, and in the end, after years of work, he revealed it in a statement which summarizes all his labours, namely, that man is needed *to illuminate the obscurity of the Creator*. His desire was to project the light of consciousness into the bottomless sea of the Unconscious, which is to say, into God himself. This is the living myth which Jung has passed down to modern man, although it is not, of course, for all men.

In the Jungian sense, the projection of consciousness is not the equivalent of reasoning; rather, it is the projection of the inner light which emanates from the mysterious 'centre' of the person, allowing him to direct himself towards the kingdom of the shadows in a constantly dynamic fashion.

Jung had observed in the eyes of animals giving birth to their young an enormous suffering which seemed to represent a fear of the dark unknown. And he believed that these animals need us, that they are waiting for us to reveal to them the nature of the world and the mystery of their painful existence. We are needed because we alone can project them into the light. Thus in a word, we will become the mirror of all creation, of animal, tree, river, stone and, perhaps, of God himself, for in the end, we are the consciousness of the world and the reflection of the flower. Nature has created us only after aeons of time so that we may in turn contemplate it in all its evanescence and reveal it in its totality. All of the elements of natural creation are sacramental objects, waiting for us to approach.

Still, for the most part, we pass by in ignorance; we pass by without *seeing* and without *looking*, in the sense that Krishna Murti gives to these words—that is, we fail to *see* and *look* with both the Conscious and the Unconscious. We pass by without knowing that the flower screams with pain out of wanting to be looked at, that the frying pan is waiting for our morning greeting, that the sun needs us to help it stay in the sky, and that the earth has asked us to help it as it rotates. But when we really *look* at the flower it greets us in response and returns us a form of love—perhaps not immediately, but at least when we ourselves dissolve into the earth. In his *Duino Elegies*, Rilke wrote something that both Jung and Hesse would have subscribed to:

> But because being here amounts to so much, because all
> this Here and Now, so fleeting, seems to require us and strangely
> concerns us. Us the most fleeting of all. Just once,
> everything, only for once. Once and no more. And we, too,
> once. And never again. But this
> having been once on earth—can it ever be cancelled?
>
> These things that live on departure
> understand when you praise them: fleeting, they look for
> rescue through something in us, the most fleeting of all.
> Want us to change them entirely, within our invisible hearts,
> into—oh, endlessly—into ourselves! Whoever we are.
> Earth, isn't this what you want: an invisible
> re-arising in us? Is it not your dream
> to be one day invisible? Earth! invisible!
> What is your urgent command, if not transformation?[1]

Man is a product of Nature; nevertheless, he rebels against it because it does not seem to accept him. This is undoubtedly due to another force which also exists in Nature and which pushes us towards sacrifice and rebellion. Nevertheless this force is but a phase or an aspect of the central force which urges us towards love. I know that this is truly the central force of nature, because when I was a child, I was able to live in perfect ease with the natural world which surrounded me. Nevertheless, in addition to the joyful God there may also be a sad God who is really waiting for us to reveal the depths of his joys and griefs. As the alchemists used to say, 'Man must finish the work which Nature has left incomplete.'

Teilhard de Chardin wrote:

'Whoever finds Jesus hidden in the creative forces of the earth will be held up in the maternal arms of Earth itself to see the face of God,' He also said: 'Whoever finds Jesus hidden in the forces of the earth that lead it to death, when he dies will be held up by the maternal arms of Earth itself and wake in the bosom of God.'

[1] Rainer Maria Rilke, *Duino Elegies* (Ninth Elegy), translated by J. B. Leishman and Stephen Spender, New York, W. W. Norton and Company, 1939.

According to Rilke, each of us will carry forth from the earth a few words, or perhaps only a single word like 'bridge', 'fountain', 'amphora' or 'fruit tree'. Each of us will bring with him the word that he loved most, and he will also bring a sprig of blue or yellow gentians. This then seems to me the Myth for modern man which Jung uttered at the end of his life and exemplified in all his work.

Yet for me, there is something more—an ultimate flower, perhaps, the flower of pure creation, which is perhaps not a natural flower at all, but one which is entirely mythical. This is the flower which Jung placed in the magic tradition that has passed down through the ages. This non-existent flower is what Jung himself called the Self, that circle whose circumference has no bounds and whose centre is to be found in no particular place. That centre in the person must be invented, because although it is there, it has never been realized; it exists only in potential. That this is not an abstruse concept will be realized when we consider our ideas of eternity and immortality, which are things which we have invented. Even the soul is something created by man. Thus we have to *believe* that the centre and flower exist, even though they may not, and even though they may never have. 'Blessed are they that have not seen, and yet have believed.'

This act of pure creation, of pure non-existence, would appear to be so fundamental that when it occurs, the whole of Nature responds, bowing before its power. And then a ray of light falls upon a tree to indicate that Nature has been touched in the centre of its soul.

Conclusion

ONE MORNING in the city of Almora, high in the Himalayas, I listened to my friend Bochi Sen who, with his legs crossed in the Hindu manner and wearing a cape he had brought from Spain, told me about his experience while on the Mount of Olives in the Holy Land. He was so moved by his memories that tears rolled down his brown cheeks. Bochi Sen then spoke about Dr. Jung whom he had visited many years before in Zürich. They had discussed reincarnation and Jung had said that if he had the opportunity to choose his next life, he would select the same one that he had already led.

This was a way of saying that, like Hesse, he had lived his life fully, grasping all its feeling. Both of these men found full satisfaction in their work because it was an expression of their very being. If I were to distinguish between the two, I would say that I had discovered more peace and serenity in Hesse than I did in Jung. Up until the last moment, Jung still seemed to be searching. Perhaps his was the road of the Magician who, unlike the Saint, did not yearn for fusion or for the peace of God, but preferred the eternal highway with all its unhappiness. But I cannot be certain of that.

If Jung was a man of science capable of expressing his discoveries in the ordinary language of men, he was also a strange being who narrated improbable experiences in a language that was at odds with that of official science. He gave new terms to those mysteries which emanate from the eternal tradition of man. That is the aspect of Jung which I have tried to demonstrate in this book—his place on the Aureate Chain and in the Hermetic Circle.

I realize that if I were to consider myself as part of that circle with Hesse and Jung, it would only be because I have tried to understand their messages and to tell what I saw in these two men. Our duty is not only towards things; it is also towards men, and the message must be passed on from generation to generation.